C000246064

Walk With The Wise

Tim Binder and Ron Owen

For Debra
with best wishes and
thanks for your company.

Tim Binder

Dedication

This book owes its existence to three groups of people. First, to our clients who provided the stimulus for the start of this collection. Secondly, to the many friends who have given of their time to read and comment on the book as it developed, offering us invaluable critique and suggestions, and of course to our publisher whose insights and skills brought the whole idea to fruition. And last, but not by any means least, to two wives (Col and Kim) who put up with us throughout the writing process and eventually came to believe that our regular meetings were more than an excuse for a good lunch.

First Published 2010

Copyright © Tim Binder and Ron Owen 2010

Tim Binder and Ron Owen have asserted their right under the Copyright, Designs and Patents Act, 1988, to be identified as the Authors of this Work.

ALL RIGHTS RESERVED

No part of this publication may be reproduced in any form, by photocopying or by any electronic or mechanical means, including information storage or retrieval systems, without the prior written permission of both the copyright owner and the publisher, nor be otherwise circulated in any form of binding or cover other than that in which it is published and without a similar condition being imposed on the subsequent purchaser.

Cover Illustration: © UpperCut Images. Shawn Frederick.

Published by Loose Chippings Books
The Paddocks, Chipping Campden, Gloucestershire, GL55 6AU
www.loosechippings.org

Printed in England by J F Print Limited, Sparkford

The authors have made diligent efforts to locate the copyright owners of all the reprinted text that appears in this book, but some have not been located. In the event that an excerpt has been printed without permission, the copyright owner should contact the authors c/o Loose Chippings Books, The Paddocks, Back Ends, Chipping Campden, Gloucestershire. GL55 6AU. Due acknowledgement will gladly be given in future editions.

ISBN 978-0-9554217-7-8

Preface

Quotations to help you see life differently. Quotations to help you achieve a better understanding of the choices with which life faces you. Perhaps even recognise that you have choice where you may have thought you had none. That is what our book is about. Our mentors are, in many cases, unexpected – in some cases, unlikely.

Quotations open the door we never opened into the rose garden. In creating this collection it is our hope to live up to this promise, so beautifully articulated by T S Eliot. And in each garden, a walk in which we eavesdrop on a conversation with someone with something to say. We see each quotation as opening three doors: one into the lives and characters of our authors – perhaps encouraging our readers to find out more about them; next, into our own reflections as we seek to capture the impact of the words on us – some emotion felt, some insight gained, some held value challenged, some new value embraced; and, finally, a door through which our readers may find some inspiration for choices they may be about to make.

Our starting point was a small collection of 'graffiti' which we had used in our work with clients, all of whom had just lost their jobs and were at a major crossroads in their lives. We stuck them on chart-boards, walls, cupboards and window ledges around our office for coffee-break browsing, to provoke thought and discussion about work, careers, work-life balance, the roles we play, the people we are and the people we'd like to be. Many, including ourselves, found some memorable words which stayed with them and helped them make life-choices, recover self-belief, gain a new direction in their lives and, in some cases, released from the treadmill of their jobs, rediscover who they were and what made them tick.

So we wanted to share them with a wider audience. And, we found ourselves adding to the original collection quotations which opened up new gardens, unconnected with the world of work, but relevant to the life-choices we are having to make all through our lives – about values; about love, both fulfilled and unrequited; about status and fame; about life, old age and death. Some you may recognise, others will, we hope, be new to you. Some are light-hearted, others are seriously learned; some rouse us like a war cry, others subtly undermine some prejudice; some make us smile; others invite us to take a hard look at ourselves. Not all the gardens opened up are flowering in sunshine; some face us with bare trees on a wintry day. Through the tapestry of the whole, however, there run the vibrant colours of human worth and dignity and a thread of optimism which hides at times but never disappears and is never defeated.

Not a book designed to be read in one page-turning frenzy! More a book to dip into as you would into a box of chocolates in which each mouthful offers a different flavour. Possibly a book for bedtime?

We have not attempted to write any one piece together, so our different styles and personalities are there for all to see. What we share is a set of values rooted in a belief in the worth of all human beings and the right of each of us to develop our unique potential. In today's world, when life for most of us is dominated by operational duties and activities imposed on us, not only by employers and family responsibilities, but by our own craving for 'busy-ness', it is a book to send you into reflective mode. It says:

'Slow down. Disengage for a moment. Think about life, think about you – where you have been, where you are, where you want to be. Take time out to reflect; maybe to re-appraise your life, to revalue its component parts, to distinguish the important from the trivial, the worthwhile from the dross.'

If, as a result of reading it, you have been able, even for a day, to carry out this bidding, our purpose in writing it will have been accomplished.

Tim Binder and Ron Owen
January 2010

Contents

Living in our world

Endings

and............ finally

Aspiring
Achieving
Finding Direction

These words confront us with a set of assumptions about the world we live in and what life is about. More particularly, what our own life is about; what we're here for.

Emerson offers us a definition of success which scorns the conventional. Stuart, Buckingham/Clifton and Sansom encourage us to explore and develop our unique potential. Eliot challenges us to lift our horizons beyond the mundane. Van Loon opens up a vision of a release of creative talent. Murray reminds us of the beauties to be explored in the world we live in. Keller inspires us to believe that we can, even if the hand life has dealt us tells us we can't.

There is, running through all of them, a challenge to value our potential, to understand that a powerful sense of self-belief is not a luxury for the lucky few, but lies within the grasp of each one of us. Frost reminds us that, always, we have choice. All challenge us to see the world differently.

" To laugh often and much; to win the respect of intelligent people and the affection of children; to earn the appreciation of honest critics and to endure the betrayal of false friends; to find the best in others; to leave the world a bit better, whether by a healthy child, a garden patch or a redeemed social condition; to know that even one life breathed easier because you lived. This is to have succeeded. "

Ralph Waldo Emerson

I came across these words of Emerson while I was working with people who had been made redundant. My role was to help them rebuild their careers and, in some cases, their lives. I was struck by the number of clients who had come to define themselves by their work role, whose self-respect rested heavily on their status in an organisation or their standing in a profession. Their job had given them, not merely an income, but also an identity, a view of themselves that was a reflection of the respect others paid them for being a doctor, company director, research scientist, actor, – whatever. When redundancy took away their job, such people felt naked, stripped of their self-esteem. Without a job, how could they still be worthwhile human beings?

Ralph

For them this dose of Emerson, which I had posted on my wall, challenged them to explore and rediscover (for they knew it once when they were young) what made them successful human beings as opposed to successful job incumbents.

As director of a world famous merchant bank, Paul had become pompous and disparaging of others over years in the role. But he took Emerson on board and accepted the challenge of redefining the word 'success'.

Released from the need to behave 'in role' he rediscovered his real self: a sense of humour which had been driven underground and a self-esteem which owed nothing to his place in a hierarchy which, with the distance of time, seemed increasingly of no importance. One day his wife surprised him at breakfast by saying:

'You know, for the first time in years I'm looking at the man I fell in love with and married.'

Ralph Waldo Emerson was born in Boston, Massachusetts in 1803 and died in 1882. A Harvard graduate, he became, first, a schoolteacher, then a Unitarian minister before resigning because he 'could no longer conscientiously administer the Lord's Supper.' Thereafter he focused his energy on writing, becoming famous for his poems and essays. Freedom of spirit, respect for the individual and a sense of awe and wonder at the world's mysteries are recurrent themes in his writing. A committed campaigner for the abolition of slavery, he once said: 'if Northern church people want to free slaves, sell your silver, buy them and set them free!'

Emerson coined the phrases 'Hitch your wagon to a star' and 'Fired the shot heard round the world'. He was also responsible for such wicked asides as 'The louder he talked of his honour the faster we counted our spoons'.

Waldo Emerson

"You will have to decide what you want to do for or by yourself, but whether you go in for making ship models or writing songs or painting the rocks of Maine or laying out a small suburban garden, enlist right away among the humble followers of the Muses. They are very exacting teachers. But they are the most satisfactory of friends, for in return for your devotion and loyalty they will occasionally let you stroll into their own private garden and then you will catch a glimpse of a world of beauty and such perfection that those few moments will most fully compensate you for any pains you may have taken to become one of the elect who have come to understand the meaning of life at its best. "

Hendrick Willem van Loon

There was a time in France when we stopped our cycling holiday for a day or so and walked in the countryside surrounding the small town that we had arrived in the day before. The summer heat stunned the town and we sat under an oak tree in a park looking back across the quiet road to the church and chateau on the opposite side.

I had my water colours with me and decided to paint the view before me. Kim, my wife, decided to take the binoculars and go for a gentle stroll.

Coaxing a picture from a white page is all absorbing and the act became akin to a meditation. Slowly the concentration overtook all the other senses bar sight – it became a single point of focus, and the meaning of Blake's words became real to me: 'to see the world in a grain of sand and Eternity in an hour'.

How long was it that I was lost in the garden of the Muses? I don't know. Kim returned and asked: 'How's it going?' and I shot from the depths of my concentration to the surface, like a cork

released from the seabed. For moments I could not orientate myself. Why was that car driving on the wrong side of the road? Where, indeed, am I? What time is it?

In a very short time I returned to reality, and the gate in the Muses' garden swung shut. I've longed to return, but it only opens when least expected. There will be other times, other places.

Becoming absorbed in a task, whether business or leisure related, can bring you to the gate. Maybe you've had times when this has happened – the clock stops and all sense of time passing is placed on hold – you are working in a state of heightened awareness and concentration – you are 'in flow' – and when the gate closes once again the sense of something special having happened is palpable.

It's worth thinking back to these times because they are unique pointers to your 'North Star'.

Van Loon (pronounced 'loan') was born in Rotterdam in 1882. In 1902 he enrolled at Cornell University, thus beginning a love affair with the US which culminated in American citizenship in 1919. He made his mark as scholar, lecturer, journalist, broadcaster and author, a multi-talented individual who achieved a PhD at Munich with a thesis written in German and who had sufficient artistic talent to illustrate his own books. He was a correspondent during the Russian Revolution of 1905 and in Belgium in 1914, going on to become an Associate Editor of the Baltimore Sun from 1922-1923. As an academic he lectured on European History at Cornell (1915-1916) and was a professor at Antioch College Ohio (1923–1924). In 1929 he made his first broadcast and followed it, from 1932 onwards with regular broadcasts for NBC. During World War II he relayed from Boston accounts of the impact of the war on American life – a kind of Dutch-American Alistair Cooke. He also became involved in fund raising for refugees from Nazi persecution.

As an author his interests were wide-ranging: children's books, straight history, biographies of Peter Stuyvesant, Thomas Jefferson and Simon Bolivar, and an answer to Hitler's Mein Kampf *entitled* Our Battle.

Perhaps his best known work is The Story of Mankind *written primarily with children in mind. His final book,* Report to Saint Peter *was published posthumously by his son in 1947. van Loon died in Old Greenwich, Connecticut in 1944.*

Willem Van Loon

" Our deepest fear is not that we are inadequate. Our deepest fear is that we are powerful beyond measure. It is our light, not our darkness that most frightens us. We ask ourselves 'who am I to be brilliant, gorgeous, talented, fabulous?' Actually, who are you not to be? You are a child of God. Your playing small doesn't serve the world. There is nothing enlightened about shrinking so that other people won't feel insecure around you. We are meant to shine, as children do. We are born to make manifest the glory of God that is within us. It is not just in some of us, it is in everyone, and, as we let our own light shine, we unconsciously give other people permission to do the same. As we are liberated from our own fear, our presence automatically liberates others. "

Marianne Williamson

Reflect for a moment on the meaning of these words and you'll find them astonishing. They are stating that the vast differences we observe all around us in human achievement are driven by the beliefs we hold about ourselves.

The nature of those beliefs, they claim, determine whether we liberate or limit, nurture or extinguish our potential for growth. Strong words? Over the top? Perhaps exaggerating to make a point. And then I thought about people I know, and it wasn't hard to bring to mind people whose lives supported the declaration. None of them is a celebrity: none of them has appeared on television nor is likely to. But all of them have shown amazing self belief and optimism to achieve in the face of a world where the odds seemed stacked against them.

Marianne

Sometimes it's the achievement of normality when their circumstances have been abnormally cruel; sometimes it's the achievement of a goal for which they inherited the worst possible disadvantages; sometimes it is an incredible fight back from an appalling illness. So maybe it is true?

Perhaps it is in everyone to shine – provided we don't confuse shining with becoming a 'celebrity'.

I think it was a former Archbishop of Canterbury who said: 'the older I get the more I discover how extraordinary ordinary people are.'

Marianne Williamson was born in Houston, Texas in 1952, the daughter of an attorney and a full time home-maker. In her twenties, and after early jobs as a cocktail waitress and lounge singer, she came across a book by Helen Schueman called A Course in Miracles *which was to change her life. She moved to Southern California and, while working as a temp, taught Schueman's philosophy at the Los Angeles Philosophical Research Society. It was the start of a career as communicator of spiritual insights and values which continues to this day.*

Williamson rapidly developed her own unique message and built a reputation both as a writer and an inspirational speaker. As we write this, she is speaking to the world via books, newsletters, 'tweets', CD's, telecast downloads, TV interviews – in fact the total panoply of modern media. She has had an impact on the lives and thinking of many people in positions of power and influence. In addition, she has set up organisations to bring practical help to people in need: The Angel Food Service for the AIDS afflicted, the Center For Living providing home helps for the seriously ill.

Passionate about democracy, Williamson founded the American Renaissance Alliance whose aim is to reclaim for individual citizens their stake in the democratic process, which she sees as having been usurped by the big corporations. Her book titles include: Illuminata - A Return to Prayer, Healing the Soul of America, *and* A Return to Love, *from which this now famous passage is taken. She once wrote: 'You can have a grievance or a miracle, but you cannot have both'.*

W i l l i a m s o n

"
Here in a quiet and dusty room they lie,
Faded as crumbled stone or shifting sand,
Forlorn as ashes, shrivelled, scentless, dry –
Meadows and gardens running through my hand.

In this brown husk a dale of hawthorn dreams,
A cedar in this narrow cell is thrust;
It will drink deeply of a century's streams,
These lilies shall make summer on my dust.

Here in their safe and simple house of death,
Sealed in their shells a million roses leap;
Here I can blow a garden with my breath,
And in my hand a forest lies asleep.
"

Muriel Stuart: The Seed Shop

Here is a picture of unfulfilled possibilities. The author holds a handful of seeds that look so dry and lacking of any promise. Yet in this handful she sees all the beauty of the full grown and formed. Consider the potential that lies in the seed; a huge cedar comes from a fingernail-sized dry flake, yet curled within that flake is the design and plan for its eventual size.

Try looking at this in a slightly more metaphysical light – perhaps our subconscious minds are like that quiet and dusty room. Perhaps we are locked into a routine, comfortable existence;

Muriel

16

except for those thoughts of doing other things, making other plans, breaking out of the mould and startling those who know us so well?

These seeds are like our thoughts and ideas. That's why they're known as seed-thoughts. They start off in the quiet and dusty recesses of our conscious minds and we plant them in the fertile soil of our subconscious.

All of our plans and dreams start in this way; in our gardens we plant a seed and walk away safe in the knowledge that, in time, it will sprout and grow to full maturity. It will never grow to be anything else – it cannot become anything other than what it is meant to be. It's the same with the garden of our mind.

Only we can stop that seed-thought realising its destiny. We can uproot it and throw it away; we can place it in another setting, or we can neglect it completely, and it will wither away.

Young plants can also be weakened by pests, so can our dreams. How? By listening to those well-meaning people who have nothing really supportive and positive to say to us; they have to tell us how a thing can't be done.

Each time we take on board what they say we weaken the plant and its hold on life. Except for the most trusted of your friends, keep your dreams and plans to yourself.

Now, starting today, how about planting some good seeds?

Muriel Stuart was born in Norbury, London, in 1885. Her father was a barrister of Scottish ancestry, which later allowed the very Scottish poet, Hugh MacDiarmid, to welcome her as an honorary Scot in one of his anthologies. She published five poetic works between 1916 and 1927, including a moving war poem, 'Forgotten Dead I Salute You'. In the remaining forty years of her life she wrote little poetry, devoting her energy to other things. In 1935 she wrote a West End play, 'The Marriage Bond', which was later made into a film by Ealing Studios. She also worked on a biography of Keats, which was never published. She co-founded the PEN Club, and married Arthur Board, a publisher, by whom she had a son and a daughter. But the love of her life was gardening, about which she wrote prolifically in her later years. A committed campaigner for female equality, she called for an end to what she saw as the deep rooted antagonism between the sexes. Stuart died in 1967 at the home of her daughter in Lyme Regis.

> " Here were decent, godless people:
> Their only monument the asphalt road
> And a thousand lost golf balls. "

T S Eliot: The Rock

These words of Eliot can be seen as a cynical reflection on the banality of life in Middle England, which they are. But they can also be taken as a challenge when we are faced with decisions which will later – perhaps much later – define the impact we make on the human landscape through which we travel in our lives. Some of the choices we make are likely to shape our 'monument'.

When the British royal family decided to stay in London during the bombing of World War II when they could have accepted any number of safe havens abroad, they shaped a monument of respect for George VI, for Elizabeth II and the entire institution of monarchy in the UK. I believe our perception of the monarchy today would be radically different if they had decided to emigrate.

When Rachmaninov decided to take up composing again, after disastrous reviews of his first symphony had plunged him into a sterile depression from which he recovered only with psychiatric help, he created the 'monument' of his best loved and most enduring works.

T   *S*

On a less spectacular level, millions of us every year face the issue of what to do with the rest of our lives – what job, what career, what educational course, what business to be in, where to invest our time, our talent, our energy.

Eliot's words challenge us to think, not only of the short term profit and loss account but of what 'monument' we will be fashioning for ourselves and what epitaph might be inscribed on it.

And when we have thought that one through, perhaps we need to ask: 'Is that really what I want?'

Thomas Stearns Eliot was born in St. Louis, Missouri, in 1888, his ancestors having emigrated from Somerset in 1670. Shortly after completing his degree at Harvard he set off on his travels to Europe – Paris, Germany, Oxford and London, where he settled down and married an English woman.

After early jobs as a schoolteacher and work in a bank, he found his metier in publishing, became editor of The Criterion *and, in 1925, joined what is now* Faber and Faber. *In 1927 he became a British citizen and was later to describe himself as 'classicist in literature, royalist in politics and Anglo-catholic in religion'. In his time he was attacked by critics for his elitism and pessimistic view of the world – and, in the USA, for being anti-American.*

We are indebted to him not only for poems such as Waste Land *but also dramas like* Murder In The Cathedral *and, of course,* Old Possum's Book Of Practical Cats *from which sprang the musical,* Cats.

He died in London in 1965 and is buried in the village of his ancestors, East Coker in Somerset.

" Life is a great network of possibilities consisting of grasped opportunities and of pitfalls for all participants. Every entity, every act, is part of the great manifestation. Every living thing adds its note, its song, its contribution through every moment of its existence. As we live our lives we leave our mark. Whatever the world may be like a hundred years from now, it will be influenced in part by what each one of us has been, has done and thought. "

Helen Nearing

What a wonderful description of a well-lived life – doesn't it resonate in you when you read that last sentence?: 'Whatever the world may be like a hundred years from now, it will be influenced in part by what each one of us has been, has done and thought.'

This is planting seeds on a planetary scale. This is making each moment count. Each day becomes something worth living if we see that what we've been, done and thought leaves its mark, for good or ill, somewhere on the greater future.

My mentor once said that living life was like walking along a gently curving path – if you stopped and looked ahead, it curved gently away so that you couldn't quite see the destination; if you looked back, it also curved gently away so that you couldn't quite see where you'd been. But then as you're bumbling along the path you suddenly come up against a big red button that just about fills the width of the path.

Helen

The button represents opportunities, possibilities, dreams, aspirations, nudges and risk. "You have a choice," he would say. "Either you suck your gut in and squeeze past the button and carry on as normal, opting for safety; or, you hit that button, and like the tilt mechanism on a pin-ball machine it will smack you off in a new direction.

You'll never know what the old path would have been like, but what you will find is that the new path will curve away gently into a land of new experiences – so hit the button boy, always hit the button!"

He never promised that life would be an unending litany of good and wonderful things – of course there will be the pitfalls and rocks – but the bumps are what we climb on and because of them we find that we progress and having come through, we are stronger and better for it – and we will have left a mark (be it ever so small) on the world.

Go on, hit that button!

Ever heard of the 'Good Life'? The phrase was created by Helen and Scott Nearing when they went 'back to the land' and were in the vanguard of the self-sufficiency movement.

Born Helen Knothe in 1904 she grew up in an economically well-off family who followed Theosophy. She joined J Krishnamurti as one of his followers before meeting and marrying the socialist economist Scott Nearing. They started the back-to-the-land movement in 1932 when they moved to a Vermont farm to begin a life of what they called 'voluntary simplicity' – reducing their needs to a minimum, growing their own food, providing for themselves and keeping things simple.

Their book Living the Good Life *became such a success that they and their farm were inundated by people who were searching for the voluntary simplicity that the Nearings had found.*

The quotation above is taken from her book Loving and Leaving The Good Life *which details her life with Scott Nearing and his voluntary death some 18 days after his 100th birthday.*

Helen died in 1995 as a result of a car accident. She was 91.

N e a r i n g

> " And if you cannot work with love but only with distaste, it is better that you should leave your work and sit at the gate of the temple and take alms of those who work with joy. "

Kahlil Gibran: The Prophet

I remember being promoted from a job I did 'with love' to a role I could only carry out 'with distaste'. The first had all the elements I enjoy about work: people centred, stimulating colleagues, worthwhile goals, busy-ness, variety and a constant sense of contributing something of value. The promotion was to a head office role where the real issues were dealt with by people reporting to me and my job was to monitor, second-guess, authorise and play whatever political games were needed. I had the big office, the status car, the place in the hierarchy and, of course, the money. They had the fun. It turned out to be a bum deal!

Kahlil

I lost the feeling of excitement as I got up in the morning, and in the evening, the sense of fulfilment as I looked back on what I had contributed that day. It was a priceless learning experience. I ended up knowing myself more deeply than ever before. Above all, after a short spell 'taking alms at the gate of the temple' (it was called Jobseeker's Allowance) I found a role which has turned out to be the most satisfying of all the many jobs I've had in a long career.

And I'm just a little proud that, since then, I have said 'no' three times to offers which were rich in salary and status but promised to be poor in terms of what I really want – need, even – from the world of work.

Next time you are offered a new job, read Kahlil Gibran's chapter on Work before accepting! And ponder on the words of Albert Camus: 'Without work all life goes rotten, but when work is soulless, life stifles and dies.'

Kahlil Gibran was born in Bisharri, a small mountain village in Lebanon, in 1883. In 1895 his family, who were Maronite Christians, emigrated to the USA where they set up a hardware store in Boston. He first achieved fame as a writer in Arabic and as a painter – his work was exhibited alongside paintings by Bonnard, Cézanne and Pissarro. Later he turned to writing in English and produced his greatest work, The Prophet, *in 1923. His own summary of it was: 'You are far greater than you think and all is well.'*

He died of cancer in 1931. The people of New York held a two day vigil for him and the New York Sun *wrote ' a prophet is dead.' He was buried in Bisharri and money from his will was used to buy a monastery in Lebanon and to raise a fund to make his homeland a place its young would not have to leave.*

G i b r a n

> Assumption A: each person's greatest room for growth is in the areas of his/her greatest weakness.
>
> Assumption B: each person's greatest room for growth is in the areas of his/her greatest strength.

Marcus Buckingham and Donald Clifton:
Now Discover your Strengths

When I first read *Now Discover Your Strengths*, I came to two immediate and disturbing conclusions. The first, that every organisation I have ever worked for operates on the basis of Assumption A; the second, that Assumption A is wrong and B is right.

Some years ago I met William. He was hired by a global finance company as an internal consultant and was an instant success: a brilliant analyst, a creative thinker, a persuasive ideas champion capable of thinking the unthinkable. So the company put him on a fast-track programme to become one of their Chief Executives. But first, those 'areas for development' – accounting, information technology, office administration, procurement etc.

He hated but endured it. Finally, appointed Chief Executive, he found himself involved in a whole range of tasks that bored him and at which he was no more than competent. He lost his joy

B u c k i n g h a m

in coming to work and his sparkle: the company lost an outstanding consultant and gained a Chief Executive who fell asleep during his Finance Director's weekly reports.

What they had done was the equivalent of an orchestra taking a brilliant pianist/composer and rotating him around his 'weak' areas – the oboe, the ticketing office, and logistics – instead of helping him grow from competent to excellent and from excellent to sublime as a creator/ performer.

If, like me, you have received a plethora of advice encouraging you to spend time and energy on developing skills at which you will never be more than OK, consider whether it would be more worthwhile investing where you know you can achieve excellence.

Clifton and Buckingham asked three thousand people the question: 'At work, do you have the opportunity to do what you do best every day?' Only twenty percent ticked 'strongly agree'.

Marcus Buckingham was born in Hertfordshire in 1966. As a schoolboy he stammered badly and was cruelly teased. He fought his handicap successfully by concentrating on things he did well – in particular, cricket and hockey – and, in this way, built up his self-esteem and confidence.

In 1987 he graduated with a Cambridge Masters degree in Social and Political Science and joined the Gallup organisation. For the next seventeen years he made the study of excellence a major part of his professional life, interviewing and studying people who were good at what they did.

This experience led him, with his mentor, Donald Clifton, to articulate a new way of developing people which they call the 'strength revolution': our quotation captures the heart of it – it is the transformation from the traditional Assumption A to the revolutionary Assumption B that the authors see to be the key to growing and releasing talent.

Through their book they have helped thousands to a new concept of personal growth and renewed belief in their capacity to achieve.

Now an independent consultant, Buckingham is a motivational speaker who regularly champions his ideas to business leaders.

a n d   C l i f t o n

"
Of all the snowflakes floating there –
The million million in the air –
None is the same. Each star
Is newly forged, as faces are,
Shaped to its own design
Like yours and mine.
And yet… each one
Melts when its flight is done;
Holds frozen loveliness
A moment, even less;
Suspends itself in time –
And passes like a rhyme.
"

Clive Sansom: Snowflakes

A powerful hymn to Uniqueness. A heartening affirmation that the Great Intelligence which set in motion the multi-billion processes of creation that happen every day in our universe means us to be special.

It didn't have to be that way. The creation of life could have been like the production of cars – easier, cheaper, and more efficient to make us standard. 'Any colour you like provided it's black' as Henry Ford is reputed to have said.

Clive

But the natural processes of creation have always been designed to avoid reproducing the identical – even identical twins are not identical, ask their mothers! The ritual dance of genetic selection that takes place when male sperm meets female egg is infallibly choreographed to ensure that each of us has his/her unique DNA and, consequently we each possess our own face, voice, walk, brain, temperament, sense of humour, trigger points for tears and laughter ….. and talent. And the same care in the avoidance of replication is apparent in all other forms of life.

To me, sheep are identical if their wool is the same colour: to shepherds, each one has its own individual face and personality. The logic of this grand design, it seems to me, is that developing our personality and our talent to their maximum potential not only offers us one of the most exciting challenges available to us, but brings us closer to achieving some kind of purpose in life.

What we do with the talent we have grown opens another chapter!

Clive Sansom was born in 1910 and lived the first forty years of his life in the UK. At the age of forty, he emigrated to Tasmania and, from there, wrote pieces celebrating his English and religious heritage. Among his poems, The Witness *won the poetry prize for the Festival of Britain in 1951.*

Sansom was a man of many parts and talents: he practised as a speech therapist but also made his mark as an anthropologist and composer, and will be remembered most durably as a poet. A profoundly religious man he found his spiritual home among the Quakers.

He died in 1981, leaving us, among many others, with a little gem of a poem called Snowflakes, *of which this quotation forms the final lines.*

Sansom

" Until one is committed there is hesitancy, the chance to draw back, always ineffectiveness. Concerning all acts of initiative and creation, there is one elementary truth, ignorance of which kills countless ideas and splendid plans: that the moment one commits oneself, then Providence moves too. All kinds of things occur to help one that would not otherwise have occurred. A whole series of events issues from the decision, raising in one's favour all manner of unforeseen incidents, and meetings and material assistance, which no man could have dreamt would have come his way. I have a deep respect for one of Goethe's couplets 'Whatever you can do, or dream you can, begin it, Boldness has genius, power, and magic in it.' "

W H (Bill) Murray

A survey asked people in the UK if they ever dream of changing their careers. It brought some interesting insights. Two thirds of the respondents said they would change their careers tomorrow if money worries and other commitments didn't stand in their way. One in five would choose a totally different career; some would go abroad to work or just travel, others would study or become full time parents/homemakers.

Some felt that they were too old to start over again; more than fifty percent felt that winning the lottery was the factor that would enable them to follow their dreams. For others only a life changing event such as redundancy or the death of someone close would spur them into action. It seems that a 'good enough' life will do and dreams must remain just that, dreams.

We mustn't be too hard on those who prefer the safer more 'secure' option. We don't know their innermost reasons but fear of the unknown is likely to be their predominant emotion, and uncertainty its partner. When there's nothing to hang on to the ride is scary. But there are the others, and we all know of them. They're the ones for whom life is an adventure. They understand that they are in charge of things; when they look back over their lives they always seem to have done or become something that they had thought about doing or becoming.

They are out there living their dreams; answering those nudges and prompts that remind us that we're off centre, that we're not integral, that there must be more to life than 'this' – whatever 'this' may be. They are inspiring and in all probability they don't realize it. They're just doing what they know they have to do, and they love it.

We are always at a point of choice. We can run with those who are shaking life by the scruff of the neck or we can loiter with the others for whom life is something they'll do after they win the lottery, retire, or when the company makes them redundant.

Ever thought who you would rather be around?

William Hutchinson Murray was a legend to the mountaineering and conservation communities worldwide. Educated at Glasgow Academy, he was originally destined for a career in banking. Then he discovered mountains and nature's great wildernesses and made them the passion of his life. In World War II he fought with the Eighth Army in North Africa where, at Mersa Matruh in 1942, he was taken prisoner. It was in German prisoner-of-war camps that he wrote, on toilet paper, his first and most influential book. When his first draft was seized and destroyed by the Gestapo, who suspected it contained a secret code, he simply started again, this time concealing the paper in his tunic. Mountaineering in Scotland *was published in 1947. It became a Bible for mountaineers and conservationists across the world. After the war, Bill resumed his climbing career and, in addition to his mountaineering books, he also wrote fiction and a history of Rob Roy MacGregor, later turned into a Hollywood film. In 1947 he married Anne, herself a mountaineer and poet, who completed his posthumously published autobiography, entitled* The Evidence of Things Not Seen. *Bill died in 1996 but his influence on conservation battles and a new generation of mountaineers is profound and enduring. In his last message to the world he wrote: 'I was lucky to view the world earlier, when more was unspoiled, untouched. Looking back over a wide landscape, cloud shadows racing over the mountain, sun, wind, I know that I have known beauty. Above all persist.'*

(B i l l) M u r r a y

" Two roads diverged in a yellow wood,
And sorry I could not travel both
And be one traveller, long I stood
And looked down one as far as I could
To where it bent in the undergrowth;

Then took the other, as just as fair,
And having perhaps the better claim,
Because it was grassy and wanted wear;
Though as for that the passing there
Had worn them really about the same.

And both that morning equally lay
In leaves no step had trodden black.
Oh, I kept the first for another day!
Yet knowing how way leads on to way,
I doubted if I should ever come back.

I shall be telling this with a sigh
Somewhere ages and ages hence:
Two roads diverged in a wood, and I –
I took the one less travelled by,
And that has made all the difference. "

Robert Frost: The Road Not Taken

R   o   b   e   r   t

This is a bit like life. Frost's words sum up what most of us do at some time or another – dwell in the lands of "What if…" and "Why didn't…". We are pretty good at beating ourselves up for not having taken another path, or regretting the one we have taken. "What if I had worked harder at school?" "Why didn't I choose another career?" "What if I'd stayed in that relationship?" or "Why didn't I get out sooner?" The questions go on and on for as long as we allow them to.

But that's the value of 20/20 hindsight. We can't do much about it now, so why not make the best of where we are?

Frost describes the other road as it turned away in the woods; it wasn't much different from the one he was on. But if he took it, it would lead him on to places where the other path could never go.

Consider this. If you had made just one different decision in your past do you think that you would be where you are now? You'll never know, but the chances are excellent that you will be somewhere else. You could say that where you are at this moment is a given. You can't change it. Your thoughts, decisions and actions in the past have brought you here. You might as well accept that as a fact. But does it mean that you are helpless to change anything? No, we're always at a moment of choice.

Think about it. You have the utmost freedom in this split-second. Whatever you say, think or do will affect the next split-second and that will affect the next and so on and on it goes. Each time that happens the road diverges.

So we're walking along the path that we've chosen to walk, and in some ways the path diverges whenever we make a decision. We'll never know what the consequences will be and that's the wonderfully exciting, and also frightening, thing about the process.

The next time the road diverges for you, why not think about taking the one less travelled?

This San Francisco-born poet was probably the leading 20th century American poet. His life was punctuated with episodes of grief and loss, and he suffered from recurring bouts of depression. He travelled to England in 1912 and made a fast friendship with the poet Edward Thomas who was killed in the Great War. This was a fruitful time for Frost and he wrote some of his best poetry whilst in England. He was a four times Pulitzer Prize winner. At the age of 86, in 1961, he spoke at the inauguration of President Kennedy. He died in 1963 and his epitaph reads: "I had a lover's quarrel with the world".

> " When one door of happiness closes, another opens; but we often look so long at the closed door that we do not see the one which has been opened for us. "

Helen Keller

These words are easy to trot out, not so easy to live. The view over our shoulder when we move towards something new is always clearer and laced with the possibility of regret and "what if?"

Whilst going through a box of family photographs, I came across a couple of pictures taken in the 1960's as my parents and siblings waited to board the ship that would take them to Australia.

They stood on the quayside in a line of people who were also leaving a grey homeland for a sunburnt country. The expressions on their faces ranged from the resigned, "I don't want to go, but what option do I have?", through the "What on earth have I done?", and into the wide-eyed, "This is going to be a big adventure" variety. My mother, who wasn't keen on leaving her friends and home in England, wore the first; my father carried the middle one, and my siblings were the wide-eyed ones.

My mother recalled the ship casting off and the passengers crowding the guard rails trying to pick out the faces of their loved ones on the quayside. Paper streamers were hurled down in the hope that they would be caught by the right person on the quayside; as if they could hold back the inevitable.

This was the last contact; the last physical link between two people. Then slowly, as the ship moved from the quayside, the streamers tautened and finally broke. Contact was lost. In an hour or so the ship was gone from sight and those on the shore had returned to their old lives and into their new roles as memories.

When we move away from the comfortable and the known, we desperately want to hold on to something familiar and safe. The future is a mystery and probably a little frightening; the present is painful, and only the past holds any comfort for us. And yet, inexorably, we move from one to the other; we can no more prevent this than we can hold back a liner with a ribbon of coloured paper.

Helen

There will come a time when the past fades from view, and as it does, you'll see the distant blue shape of your goal coming closer, and soon you'll find yourself standing on the shore you had dreamed of all that time ago.

Before setting out on the next stage of your personal voyage how about spending some time thinking deeply about how you would like your new experience to be?

Helen Keller was born in Tuscumbia, Alabama in 1880. At the age of nineteen months she contracted an illness which left her blind and deaf. From that moment her life developed into an amazing struggle in which, with the help of companions and mentors, she overcame impossible odds to become an acclaimed writer, campaigner, public speaker and inspiration to millions around the world.

A film, The Miracle Worker, *celebrated her life and achievements. Any one of the learning challenges she tackled was daunting enough on its own: communication by touch, reading Braille in four languages (French, German, Greek, and Latin), voice production. Yet she not only mastered the skills but used them to make an impact on twentieth century America and beyond.*

She was the first deaf-blind person to achieve a BA; she wrote twelve books and numerous articles; she campaigned for women's rights and better conditions for the poor; she became an active member of the Socialist party; she appeared on vaudeville shows to promote the cause of the blind; she counted among her friends the likes of Charlie Chaplin, Jascha Heifetz, Sophie Tucker and Enrico Caruso; and she was received by every US president from Grover Cleveland to John F Kennedy. She once said: 'I do not want the peace that passeth understanding, I want the understanding that bringeth peace.'

Before she was two, life had cruelly closed on her the doors of sight and sound: by her own resilience, determination and self-belief she opened up others so successfully that, near the end of her life, she could say 'I believe that through these dark and silent years God has been using my life for a purpose I do not know … but, one day I shall understand and then I will be satisfied.'

Helen Keller 'drifted off in her sleep' on 1ˢᵗ June 1968.

> **"** The violets in the mountains have broken the rocks. **"**

Tennessee Williams

Billy was from the other side of the tracks, black, poor and abandoned by his father when he was a child. He had been on Death Row in Texas for 18 years when he came into my life. I had joined an organisation which was dedicated to arranging pen-pals for those awaiting execution. Billy and I began corresponding and a relationship developed that turned my view of life and the world on its head.

One of my letters asked Billy what he could see from his cell window. He replied 'Nothing. Only sky and razor wire'. But that letter was closely followed by another saying that he had seen a red bird sitting on the wire, and did I know what it was?

Turns out it was a Cardinal; I let Billy know and gave him some details. His reply came back with a strange request: 'What does grass feel like under your feet?' Good question. Try explaining the coolness, the tickle and the 'give' of it as you step on it.

Another letter and another request: 'What does a tree feel like?' That took me into the local park and the nearby arboretum. The bark of a Silver Birch was smooth and warmed from the sun. The deep spiralling runnels in a Sweet Chestnut took my fingertips up to the first joint. The soft, deep russet bark of the Sequoia gave under the pressure of my hand.

Then, a letter of wonder: "How can something as soft as a flower, push its way through concrete?" He explained that, in the exercise yard he had found a small flower that had indeed broken through the surface.

In time I visited this gentle black man with a soft voice and beautifully manicured hands. He told me about his background and how he came to be on the 'Row' at seventeen and how he felt it wouldn't be long before 'the State killed' him. Then his date was set; he didn't see the year out.

Billy's final letter arrived a day after he was executed asking if we could look upon him as our son. It was too late to do anything but inwardly say 'Of course'. My last letter was returned with 'Deceased' scrawled untidily across it.

34

What came out of the correspondence was the unfailing strength of the human spirit of one indigent black man who rose above the system and gave a whole new sense of wonder to someone living in a distant country. I don't think that's bad for someone the State had given up on.

Thomas Lanier Williams was born in Columbus, Mississippi in 1911, into a family with more than its fair share of interpersonal tensions. His father, a travelling salesman, was described as crude, stingy and drunken; his mother overcompensated with a 'smothering' love: his sister Rose was a schizophrenic who was subjected by her parents to a lobotomy. 'Not a pleasant refuge' was how Williams described his home and he turned elsewhere for support – to his grandparents in his youth and later to Frank Merlo, an ex-US Navy mariner, his partner from 1947 to 1963, when Frank died of cancer.

His deep southern drawl earned him the nickname 'Tennessee' from his fellow students at Washington University, St. Louis, Missouri, a name he took into personal ownership for the rest of his life. He left Washington after the first year but later graduated from the University of Iowa in 1938. Williams wrote prolifically from an early age – poems, one-act plays, short stories, two novels and, of course, the full-length plays for which he is famous. Of these, four have proved enduringly popular and relevant with the passage of time: Glass Menagerie (1945), A Streetcar Named Desire (1947), Cat on a Hot Tin Roof (1955), and Night of the Iguana (1961).

Critics argue over whether particular characters are depictions of members of his dysfunctional family. He once confessed 'I write from my own tensions – for me, this is a form of therapy.' Much of the power of his writing comes from the sad intensity of his own experiences – a homosexual in a society which dare not speak the name, addicted to drugs and alcohol. Little wonder that he focused on 'the faded and frightened and difficult and odd and lonely.' He once wrote: 'there are two kinds of people who live outside this so-called world of ours – the artists and the insane.'

On 24th February 1983 he was in the process of putting in his eye drops, head back and with the bottle cap held between his teeth. The cap slipped into his throat, choking him. A bizarre and tragic end to a turbulent, creative life.

W i l l i a m s

> " You are a child of the universe, no less than the trees and the stars. You have a right to be here. "

Max Ehrmann: Desiderata.

Thirty years ago I left a marriage that wasn't working. It was the most difficult and painful decision I have made in my life; it meant living apart from my children who were then eight and twelve. I will never forget the guilt, feeling it deep in my bones, breathing it in the very air of the London suburb where I had moved into a 'student' bed-sit. Every time I saw parents taking their kids to school or playing with them in a park I was brought to the brink of tears. I felt like the worst of criminals because I had caused this trail of pain across three lives – and for what? For whom? What gave me the right to do such a thing?

It was at this point that I revisited Desiderata.

'You are a child of the universe no less than the trees and the stars. You have a right to be here.'

And, Ehrmann said to me, a right to be a happy and complete human being instead of a wounded martyr, to enjoy a loving, liberating relationship instead of an unrewarding compromise, to have in my life the invigorating force of joy instead of mere absence of aggravation. His voice called out to

M a x

me above the sounds of disapproval from people who could only focus on the negative effects of marriage break-up. I felt he was saying:

'Take the pain and fight through it to become what you have a right to be.'

So I did. And I didn't look back.

The universe, the trees and the stars were on my side. And, thankfully, so, in the long run, were my kids.

Max Ehrmann was born in Terre Haute, Indiana, of Bavarian immigrant parents in 1872. He went to De Pauwe University and, later, Harvard, where he completed a post-graduate degree in Law and Philosophy.

Meanwhile, his spiritual education was being provided by the German Methodist Church. He became Deputy State Attorney and then went on to serve as a lawyer to the family manufacturing business.

At the age of forty he decided to devote his full-time energy to writing and publishing articles, essays, drama and poetry. He is best remembered for Desiderata *from where this quotation is taken; Warner Brothers issued it as a single record in 1971 even though it was originally written in 1926!*

It is, however, another poem which earns him a place in Best Poems Of The American People. *One that contains the lines:*

'May I not forget that poverty and riches are of the spirit…

Give me a few friends who love me for what I am…

May the evening's twilight find me gentle still..'

" Il dépend de celui qui passe que je sois tombe ou trésor, que je parle ou me taise. Ceci ne tient qu'a toi, ami: n'entre pas sans désir.

It depends on whoever passes by whether I become a tomb or a treasure, whether I speak or hold my peace. It is up to you my friend: do not enter here without desire. "

Words inscribed on the Palais de Chaillot, Paris.

The words look down on a turmoil of tourists and street vendors milling about on the steps and terraces in front of the Palais. There is a market of ambulant salesmen touting mechanical birds, plastic replicas of the Eiffel Tower, sunglasses when it's bright and umbrellas when it's raining. It is rare to catch anyone looking up to read the inscription.

At first sight it seems that the kind of 'désir' which the writer wants to be our entry fee, is a commodity in short supply. Any one word sells 'désir' short. 'Thirst for knowledge' gets close, but it lacks the sense of passionate curiosity which is not satisfied until it has achieved a genuine and empathic understanding.

There are people who have travelled the world, who take with them such little passion for discovery that their minds and imaginations come back no richer than when they set out. And there

P a l a i s

are those like Charles Darwin, who took his curiosity to the Galápagos Islands and revolutionised the way we think about the origins of our world. Why such a difference? Are we born with or without hunger for knowledge? Or does it depend on the kind of teachers we had in our early years at school?

In today's environment, choosing a school for our children is likely to be hugely influenced by the answer to the question: 'What are their exam results?' Maybe a more important question is: 'Does it have teachers capable of developing in my kids that most precious of legacies, a lifelong love of exploration, a quest for knowledge, the joy of discovery?'

Or, as the Palais de Chaillot has it: 'désir'?

The Palais de Chaillot was built in 1937 to celebrate the French Empire and remains as a monument to an age when the great European powers competed with each other to rule large portions of the world.

It takes its name from the hill on the bank of the Seine immediately opposite the Eiffel Tower, and is now a complex of theatre and museum. It houses the French National Navy Museum and the Museum of Mankind.

The words are unattributed and our research has so far failed to identify an author.

de Chaillot

Loving and Relating

In this section our authors have things to say to us about our relationships with other people. They focus our attention on love – its power, its quirkiness, its tendency to possess, its potential to devastate. When it is not returned, do we write a lament as in Thomas Hardy, or take what comfort we may from 'love without hope' as in Robert Graves?

Betjeman challenges us to ponder the power of love to transform human beings. Greene and Blake in their different ways warn us against the temptation to control and manipulate those we love. And, if we imagine that love is only for the young, we should read Bourdillon and Browning. Are strangers comfortably outside the pale of our responsibility? Or does Jenny Cohen's epitaph stir us to move the fence?

All manner of events and human reactions stay stubbornly out of our control. For instance, when someone dumps us, we feel we have lost control completely. But in the way we perceive the person and the event, and in the way we respond, we always have a choice. To reach this insight will, for many of us, involve seeing life differently.

66 The night has a thousand eyes,
And the day but one;
Yet the light of the bright world dies
With the dying sun.

The mind has a thousand eyes,
And the heart but one;
Yet the light of a whole life dies
When love is done. 99

F W Bourdillon

How do you define love? We use the word so loosely. We love the wife; we love lemon meringue pie; we love rock music; if we are obedient Christians, we love the Lord our God with all our heart and we love our neighbours as ourselves.

When Prince Charles was asked, in a famous television interview, whether he and Diana were in love, he answered, somewhat hesitantly, 'Yes – whatever love means.'

So, what sort of love is it that provides 'the light of a whole life' which 'dies when (it) is done'? I suspect we all have different answers to this question, individually shaped in the forge of our life experiences. For some of us love is inseparable from physical attraction and desire; for others its crowning glory is expressed in the unconditional love of a parent for a child. Maybe it can't be defined but only described?

F   W

'When some person becomes more important to you than life itself' is one attempt at a description. If this gets to somewhere near the truth, does it not follow that to cherish love is to cherish the people you love?

And if the experience of love is missing from your life, does it not follow that you must search, not for love, but for people?

Born in Sussex in 1852, Francis William Bourdillon was educated at Haileybury and Worcester College, Oxford.

He made his mark as a scholar, private tutor and poet. As a scholar, he translated medieval French literature; as a tutor, he coached aspiring university entrants, including the sons of Prince Christian of Schleswig Holstein; and as a poet he published Among the Flowers, A Lost God, Sursum Corda, Preludes and Romances, *and* Christmas Roses.

He even contributed a war poem – False Gods *published in* The Times *in 1914. His poems commanded respect from reviewers and poetry lovers, but never became widely read.*

Bourdillon loved Sussex and dedicated his first book of poems, not to a person, but 'to Woolbeding' where his father was vicar. He died in the village of Buddington, near Midhurst in the county he loved, in 1921.

The Times *obituary of 14ᵗʰ January 1921 describes him as 'a minor poet of sincerity and charm, an industrious and fortunate student ...... a great lover of his friends and a most human and delightful companion'.*

B o u r d i l l o n

'Let us not speak, for the love we bear one another –
Let us hold hands and look.'
She such an ordinary little woman;
He such a thumping crook;
But both, for a moment, little lower than the angels
In the teashop's inglenook.

John Betjeman: In a Bath Teashop

They sat opposite me on the 11.28 to Waterloo. A young couple in their twenties. He had a misshapen, spotty face which, if you were a potter, you would want to break up so that you could start again. She was a roly-poly dumpling of a girl, shaped like a cottage loaf with the merest gesture in the direction of a waist. She had thick glasses and crooked teeth, and, if I had noticed either of them on their own, my instinct would have been to feel sorry for them.

But one thing changed all that: one powerful, transforming thing. They were in love. Not just 'fond of', 'good friends', but sending each other signals of in-love fascination as they held hands and canoodled, oblivious to me and everyone else on the 11.28.

For the whole of the hour long journey they traded with each other, with eyes more than words, a tenderness which excluded the rest of us and created its own special bubble. A couple in love. It made them beautiful – and gave a meaning I had not previously felt to this touching poem of Betjeman's. Short-changed on physical attractiveness, but ……….. little lower than the angels. They were unaware that, as I raised my South West Trains coffee cup to my lips, I was toasting them.

John

In a world in which our concept of beauty is being continually shaped by photographers, fashion editors and film makers it is easy to forget that the ingredients which create and nourish exciting, satisfying and durable relationships defy the camera.

'What is essential is invisible to the eye.' (Antoine de Saint-Exupéry)

Born in London in 1906, Betjeman died, after a long struggle with Parkinson's disease, in 1984. In his lifetime he became a very English national treasure. Educated at Marlborough and Magdalen College, Oxford – from which he was sent down without a degree – he was later awarded degrees by nine universities (including Oxford!).

Whilst establishing himself as a writer he did various jobs including primary school teacher, private secretary, and film critic of the Evening Standard.

His collections of poetry ranged across muscular women and padres, awful architecture, philistine business men, gas-lit Victorian churches and railway stations, shopping arcades, bogus Tudor bars, favourite places and famous people.

He discovered, well ahead of the rest of the world, the beauties of Victorian architecture. During World War II he joined the film division of the Ministry of Information and was credited with the decision to film Olivier's Henry V in Ireland, where his role was to influence the Irish in a pro-British direction. The IRA ordered his assassination but it was revoked by a senior IRA commander who liked his poetry!

After the war he developed his career as a writer, broadcaster and champion of national treasures. Philip Larkin wrote of him that he communicated 'a gaiety, a sense of the ridiculous, an affection for human beings and how and where they live, a vivid and vivacious portrait of mid-twentieth century English social life.'

Betjeman

> " Love without hope, as when the young bird-catcher
> Swept off his tall hat to the Squire's own daughter,
> So let the imprisoned larks escape and fly,
> Singing about her head as she rode by. "

Robert Graves: Love Without Hope

I had to read this poem twice before I took on board the lovely cameo it painted with the poignant frugality of its words: the village lad who had spent all day patiently baiting and finally trapping his larks; the pride and satisfaction of securing them in his tall hat; the anticipation of reward when he sold them to some affluent ladies as song birds for their loneliness; the plans he had already made to spend the money.

Then the Squire's lovely daughter rides by. And he has an impossibly difficult choice! Keep his hat on and appear discourteous and no gentleman? Or see his day's work wasted as his precious larks fly free?

So he sweeps off his tall hat – not in some fit of absentmindedness, but as the culmination of a brief but desperate struggle – and thus makes his own declaration of love to her.

Whether she noticed him or not is left for us to speculate. But the sight of them 'singing about her head as she rode by' would reward his love-struck heart above and beyond the price of larks.

Perhaps the appeal of this poem to me is that it is a hymn to the unobtainable, the dream which is forever beyond our reach and which, for that very reason, will always be there to inspire us.

As Robert Browning wrote: 'Ah, but a man's reach should exceed his grasp, Or what's a heaven for?'

Robert Graves was one of the war poets who came back.

Born in 1895, educated at Charterhouse, he joined the army in 1914 and wrote his first poem while serving in France. After the war he read English at St. John's College, Oxford but left without a degree. (Later he was awarded a B.Litt. for his thesis on Poetic Unreason.)

Between the wars, in addition to many poems, he wrote I Claudius *and* The White Goddess. *In this treatise he puts forward the view that 'true poets derive their gifts from the Muse, the primitive matriarchal Moon Goddess, female principal once dominant, now dispossessed by male values of reason and logic.'*

Graves was Professor of Poetry at Oxford from 1961 to 1966 and died in 1985.

G r a v e s

> " Grow old along with me
> The best is yet to be. "

Robert Browning: Rabbi Ben Ezra

A man aware of the approaching autumn of his life. A man at ease with his age. A man comforted by two powerful thoughts.

The first: he is not alone. He has someone to share with him chill winds and the beauty of dying leaves, ripe sunsets and the mellow dampness of meadows, stout walls and the comfort of a live fire.

The second: life has not yet given up its storehouse of joys. There is more for those who care to ask.

More – but, maybe different. Thrill of speed through the countryside replaced by unhurried appreciation of its beauty; the adrenalin of competition by the warmth of collaboration; the winning of prizes by the coaching of others; a multiplicity of future plans by a wealth of reminiscences; a ton of effort by an ounce of wisdom; possessive passion by selfless love. Different – and, maybe more!

Keep on asking: keep on demanding: the best is yet to be.

Browning was born in Camberwell in 1812. A precocious child, he began to write poetry as a boy, although he did not achieve popular fame until the 1860's. He attended Peckham School and London University but withdrew from both in favour of his father's library and the tutelage of cultured parents.

Fortunately for young Robert, his parents were wealthy and able to fund, not only an aristocratic life style of travel but also the publication of his early works.

In 1841 Elizabeth Barrett wrote to him praising his poetry. He replied: 'I love your verse with all my heart and I love you too.' They were married at St. Marylebone's church in 1846 and went to live in Italy. She died in his arms in 1861, just as his reputation was growing to celebrity status.

Browning lived on to receive national acclaim, an audience with Queen Victoria and honorary degrees at both Oxford and Cambridge. He saw his work widely quoted (a verse of his appeared on the Chicago railway timetable!) and achieved notoriety as an extravagant dresser – 'As far a dandy as a sensible man can be'.

When he died in Venice in 1889, a funeral cortege carried his body by gondola along the Grand Canal to San Michele, resting place of Italy's great and good. Later, it was transported by train to Westminster Abbey, where he now lies in Poets' Corner.

Perhaps he's best known for his memorable telling in verse of the story of the Pied Piper, and such lines as 'God's in his heaven, All's right with the world.' And 'Oh to be in England, Now that April's here.'

B r o w n i n g

> " He who binds to himself a joy
> Does the winged life destroy;
> But he who kisses the joy as it flies
> Lives in eternity's sunrise. "

William Blake: Eternity

Blake's words are a challenge, not simply to those who keep birds in cages, but to all who experience the kind of love that wants to possess the loved one; to chain and control, to organise and manipulate, to bind in service.

The controlling hand is not always obvious – it may not be engaged in bullying but instead, may have developed a hundred ways of exercising control by emotional blackmail: 'How can you do this to me?' or 'How come you didn't call me?' or 'How am I going to manage without you?'

At the heart of this love is self-love. Its owners don't love the caged bird but the sound of its singing; not what it is but what it does for them. And the problem the poet has in getting his message across is that it always resonates with the prisoner but rarely with the jailor. Not many jailors recognise what they are doing to the one they claim to love.

This means that, if anything is to change, the bird must find a way of opening the cage on its own initiative and be brave enough to fly, even without the kiss of joy!

w i l l i a m

William Blake was born in London in 1757. His father was a hosier and his mother his earliest mentor and most abiding influence. Both parents encouraged him in the direction of art as a career and saw him apprenticed as an engraver. This experience laid the foundation for his later skills as printer and painter.

As a child he had visions of angels appearing to him in the trees, and this faculty for perceiving the extra-sensory stayed with him for the rest of his life and features in many of his works both written and visual. It was probably this which caused some of his contemporaries to describe him as mad - he was certainly strange and prone to eccentric behaviour. Wordsworth said of him '...there is something in the madness of this man which interests me more than the sanity of Lord Byron and Walter Scott...'

He left many memorable gems including the lines 'To see a world in a grain of sand, And heaven in a wild flower, Hold Infinity in the palm of your hand, And Eternity in an hour.'

He died in 1827 and is buried in an unmarked grave in Bunhill Fields, London. Never rich in his lifetime, he achieved fame only after his death.

B l a k e

> " Be kind;
> for everyone you meet is fighting a hard battle. "

Inscription on the tombstone of Dr. Jenny Cohen, Highgate Cemetery.

Most of us have our favourite 'hate targets'. People who arouse the worst in us, people we find irritating and unlovable, to whom we are ready to attribute the lowest motives for everything they do. With them we are quick to anger and slow to forgive. They have a genius for pressing those buttons which turn us into curmudgeons: spend time with them and we cease to like ourselves. Sometimes it's personal. Sometimes it's the job they do – ever lost your temper with a tax inspector, traffic warden or call centre operator?

Jenny Cohen's words are a reminder that very few people set out to be gratuitously rude, unpleasant, unhelpful or stupid. Their behaviour, in all probability, makes sense to them. It's almost certainly a result of that intricate cocktail formed by their genes and upbringing shaken and stirred with the role they are called upon to play and the events and people who are currently centre-stage in their lives. I doubt if there is a person alive who would not say 'yes' to the question: are you currently engaged in some kind of battle?

We recognise and can describe too well our own battles. Perhaps the recognition that the other guys have theirs could be the onset of kindness?

My thanks to Jenny Cohen: 'a magnificent woman'- I would like to have known her.

J e n n y

Highgate Cemetery was created in 1839 (when the life expectancy of a Londoner was thirty-six years) and extended in 1854, when a tunnel was dug under Swains Lane and a hydraulic lift installed to transfer the coffins to Highgate East. A period of disuse and vandalism followed post 1945, and the cemetery was closed in 1975. It was sold to Friends of Highgate Cemetery for £50 in 1981 and has been progressively restored since then with the help of grants and volunteer labour. It is now open to the public; Highgate East (daily, free access) and Highgate West by means of guided tours.

It was designed by Stephen Geary, J B Bunning and David Ramsey as 'a beautiful resting place for the rich.' One William Mellish was transferred to Highgate from an East End burial ground in 'a touch of snobbery, a desire to be surrounded in death by richer and more interesting people than he had known in life'. In its heyday its clientele would arrive in carriages drawn by black-plumed horses, possibly accompanied by paid mourners ('mutes').

What we have today is 'a maze of rising terraces, winding paths, tombs and catacombs, a monument to the Victorian age and the Victorian attitude to death' (John Murray), a Grade II listed park, a place of outstanding historical and architectural interest, a landscape populated by the most amazing collection of Victorian sculpture.

Its rich history and visual impact has been captured by John Gay and Felix Barker in Highgate Cemetery: Victorian Valhalla. *It is the last resting place of a host of famous people, including the Rossetti family, George Eliot, Herbert Spencer, Rowland Hill, Charles Wesley, Edwin Landseer, Karl Marx and Ralph Richardson.*

And, of course, people who never achieved fame and possibly never sought it. People like Dr. Jenny Cohen, on whose tombstone someone has added: 'a magnificent woman.'

C o h e n

> " We must live for the few who know and appreciate us, who judge and absolve us, and for whom we have the same affection and indulgence. The rest I look upon as a mere crowd … from whom there's nothing to be expected but fleeting emotions … which leave no trace behind them. "

Sarah Bernhardt 1844 -1923.

I once had a client who was a senior manager for an oil company. In his gift were millions of pounds worth of supplier contracts. When he lost his job I encouraged him to seek out his network of friends and engage their support. He drew up a list of around thirty to forty and set about contacting them with a view to meeting up. Among them were people who had regularly invited him and his wife to dinner and cocktail parties and whom he counted among his friends. He was in shock when only a handful responded: the majority made their excuses. Out of his role, he was no longer of use to them, and, out of a job he was an embarrassment. He had learned, in the hardest possible way, the difference between political affiliation and friendship, between 'the mere crowd' and the people who valued him for himself.

There are those who never experience the crisis which helps us sort the one from the other: imagine how difficult it must be for a member of the royal family to know who their real friends are! When we are young we are unreasonably vulnerable to the influence of 'the mere crowd'. What we wear, our taste in music and cars, our role models, our choice of food, drink and restaurants are all conditioned by what 'They' will think about it and how we will be judged by 'Them'.

S a r a h

The crowd can be cruel – and hopelessly wrong. By the time we reach a certain age we have the evidence to sort out the People Who Matter in our lives, 'the few who know and appreciate us, who judge and absolve us, and for whom we have the same affection and indulgence.'

Once we pass this 'certain age' there's no excuse for any confusion!

She was called 'the most famous actress in the history of the world', 'the Divine Sarah' and, by Alexander Dumas (fils) 'a notorious liar'! She was the darling of the stage and the world of early silent cinema; revered from her native Paris to London, Rio de Janeiro and New York. It was in New York that she took part in the earliest experiments to record sound – on one of Thomas Edison's cylinders. She played a two minute part as Hamlet in his duel with Laertes, with Edison's cylinder providing sound effects. In her mainstream career, in films and the theatre, she played all the major female roles (and occasionally a male part!) on a stage dominated by the great dramatists – Racine, Molière, Dumas, Ibsen, Shakespeare.

She made eight motion pictures and died while filming her last, the producer having to use a body double for the final shots with her back to the camera. In 1905 she injured her right knee leaping from a wall in the play Tosca *and lost her leg as gangrene set in. This meant that for the remaining years of her career, she was immobile on stage (having rejected a prosthetic leg) dominating the stage with her magnificent voice.*

Pictures of her show a great beauty with huge dark eyes, abundant black hair and a nose which betrays her Jewish ancestry – both parents were thought to be Jewish and from Amsterdam. She had an unhappy marriage to a Greek-born actor who turned out to be a drug addict, an affair with a Belgian prince who gave her a son, and a rumoured affair with the Prince of Wales (later Edward VII). Among her friends she numbered the writer Victor Hugo, and the artists Gustave Doré and Louise Abbema.

She died of uraemia in 1923 in the care of her only child, Maurice, and is buried in the Père-Lachaise cemetery in Paris. With her looks, her contacts and her fame it could not have been easy for her to separate 'the few' from 'the mere crowd'.

B e r n h a r d t

" No human being can really understand another, and no-one can arrange another's happiness. "

Graham Greene: The Heart of the Matter

There are people in all our lives whose happiness we would love to arrange. Most commonly they are our children: because we love them, because they are pieces of us, because they 'belong' to us, because who they are is a reflection of who we are.

It can also be a partner. There are those who have entered into a relationship – a marriage, even – nurturing from the outset some ambition to 'rearrange' their other half. 'Once he's with me he'll be a different man' or, 'Before she met me she didn't know what tidy meant.'

And there are those who, like me, have been professionally engaged in coaching and counselling other people, who have faced the daily temptation to exaggerate our role in the lives of our clients, to overstep the sacred line that delineates the boundary of their right to self-governance and thus diminish their responsibility for themselves.

Graham Greene's perceptive words pour a bucket of cold reality on our well intended delusion that we can play God with other people's lives. They say: 'Back off and respect that divine right we all have to be different, to be ourselves, to be wrong.'

Sometimes the best thing we can do for those we care about is to let them go.

If any writer lived a long and full life which provided a glut of material for his novels, that man was Graham Greene. Born in Berkhamstead in 1904, he died in Switzerland in 1991. In between, he took an Oxford degree in History before embarking on a career which led him into journalism (film critic for The Spectator *among other posts) and spying – he worked for MI6 full-time at first, then later, still supplying intelligence reports long after he had become a successful writer.*

In his travels he spent time in West Africa, Vietnam, Poland, Russia, China, South America, Haiti and Cuba.

He lived in France for most of his final years. He separated from his wife in 1946 and went on to have two mistresses neither of whom ever left her husband even though, in each case, the relationship with Greene was an open secret.

For Greene, flawed characters have an endless fascination, whether they are evil, as in Pinkie in Brighton Rock, *or tortured by failure as in Scobie in* The Heart of the Matter. *The Catholic in him never allows them to escape the clutches of conscience; the compassionate human being in him causes him to strive to understand and forgive.*

He once wrote: 'The truth …. has never been of any real value to any human being – it is a symbol for mathematicians and philosophers to pursue. In human relations kindness and lies are worth a thousand truths.'

"
Perhaps, long hence, when I have passed away,
Some other's feature, accent, thought like mine,
Will carry you back to what I used to say,
And bring some memory of your love's decline

Then you may pause awhile and think, 'Poor jade!'
And yield a sign to me – as ample due,
Not as the tittle of a debt unpaid
To one who could resign her all to you –

And thus reflecting, you will never see
That your thin thought, in two small words conveyed,
Was no such fleeting phantom-thought to me,
But the Whole Life wherein my part was played;
And you amid its fitful masquerade
A Thought – as I in yours seem to be.
"

Thomas Hardy: She To Him II

T h o m a s

For the person at the wrong end of this exchange, feelings are likely to be a cocktail of grief, anger, despair and wounded self-esteem.

First reactions to the news that you have been 'dumped' are often disastrous. Some launch an immediate barrage of hatred and blame which effectively kills off hope of any kind of relationship in the future; some grovel in an attempt to win back the lost affection and, in so doing, surrender some important bastion of their personality; others, like the lass in the poem, accept their loss, grieve for it, and find ways of coping which release them to get on with their lives – in her case by writing these lovely words.

It is a sad reality that, when relationships break up, the good times are forgotten, what the couple valued about each other is rubbished and the time they spent together forming part of each other's life is regarded as wasted.

If only we could include, in the psychological contract that underpins each close relationship, words like: 'If you should one day go where I can't be, I'll cherish that of you you leave in me, And hope that you will be for ever true, To that of me that I have left in you.'

Thomas Hardy, uncrowned Poet Laureate of Wessex in perpetuity, was born near Dorchester in 1840. His early efforts at poetry failed to find a publisher but, instead of devoting himself to his day job as an architect, he wrote fourteen novels and forty short stories.

Works such as The Mayor of Casterbridge, The Woodlanders *and* Far From The Madding Crowd *made him famous in his own lifetime. But a hostile reception to* Jude the Obscure *in 1896 caused him to abandon the novel and return to poetry.*

This time, with an established reputation as a writer, he was welcomed by the publishing fraternity and enjoyed a regenerated career as a poet. He wrote productively up until the year of his death in 1928.

W.H.Auden said of him 'He was a good poet, perhaps a great one, but not too good.'

> *Under the Sea-wind* …. was written, moreover, out of the deep conviction that the life of the sea is worth knowing. To stand at the edge of the sea, to sense the ebb and the flow of the tides, to feel the breath of a mist moving over a great salt marsh, to watch the flight of shore birds that have swept up and down the surf lines of the continents for untold thousands of years, to see the running of the old eels and the young shad to the sea, is to have knowledge of things that are as nearly eternal as any earthly life can be. These things were before ever man stood on the shore of the ocean and looked out upon it with wonder; they continue year in, year out, through the centuries and the ages, while man's kingdoms rise and fall. "

Rachel Carson

I love the sea. I don't really know why but the sound and taste of it and all that implies its presence fills me with a feeling of arrival – of having come back home. Much of my childhood was spent near the sea; born in Worthing, lived in Shoreham and on the Pembrokeshire coast; holidays in Bognor Regis where pebbly days were spent, always it seems to me, crowned by the gymnastics involved in changing out of cold, wet swimming wear under a damp and sand-gritty towel.

I guess I've been lucky for I've travelled on all of the great oceans and have crashed through storms and gales on most of them. I've watched Pacific rollers beating on the Californian shoreline and sat on Cape Leeuwin (one of the world's 'Great Capes') in Western Australia watching huge Southern Ocean waves powering on their never-ending voyage around the world.

Rachel Carson also loved the sea and all that went in, on, over and around it. This passage raises such feelings in me that I still find it as evocative and moving on the 'nth' reading as I did when I first found

Rachel

it. I was a young Marine then, based in Portsmouth, and in the evening that I first read it I walked along the seashore, stumbling and slipping over the pebbles with the sound of darkened waves in my ears. All my senses were on edge and sharply honed by my having all the delicious sufferings of infatuation, so that even the barking of orders meant nothing to me providing they did not prevent me from seeing the person, who at that time, meant so very much to me.

The sea is almost an allegory for this sort of relationship – the climactic build-up, the curling over and the fall and the gentle fading out of something that was once immensely powerful. I went away from Portsmouth when the wave was at its highest; when I came back it had dissipated itself on the stones of absence and we were like two strangers.

On the last evening that we saw each other we walked by the sea and it was as still and quiet as our relationship.

The sea is a great healer – if you're troubled you could do worse than take yourself to the coast, find a sandy spot, and there, write your troubles in the sand, and then wait and watch as the sea gently erases them.

The environmental movement as we know it starts here. In 1962 Rachel Carson's book Silent Spring *challenged the agricultural scientists and the government of the day over their profligate use of synthetic pesticides and insecticides; that it hit a chord was demonstrated when it brought devastating attacks by the rich and powerful of these huge organisations crashing down on the head of the gentle woman who rang the alarm bells so loudly. She had a way with words that opened up the natural world for readers and her three books about the sea –* Under the Sea Wind, The Sea Around Us, *and* The Edge of the Sea *– brought a whole new generation into contact with the natural world. She became Editor in Chief of all publications of the US Fish and Wildlife Service during a fifteen year career with that organisation and in 1952 she resigned to devote her time to writing, producing in the process a small classic called* The Sense Of Wonder *as well as the sea books and* Silent Spring. *She died of cancer in April 1964 – leaving the world safer, our place in creation better understood, and our lives richer as a result of her writing; which is more than can be said about the critics that attacked her in the early 1960s.*

C a r s o n

Living In Our World

Our world is a baffling but intriguing jungle. Its laws are rarely fair or logical. Its inhabitants include saints and villains, babes and butchers, honest men and devious manipulators, war-mongers and peacemakers, the smart and the dumb, the beautiful and the ugly. To navigate it we all need some inner compass of values coupled with a strong sense of identity.

Our authors in this section offer us something of their own portfolio of values and insights; we don't have to agree with them but even in disagreeing we are essentially defining our own.

Mandela offers an optimistic perception of human nature at odds with the traditional Christian doctrine of original sin; Al Capp a sceptic's take on the world of art; Sitwell a critical spotlight on a generation obsessed with celebrity; Owen and Laurentin invite us to share their abhorrence of war and violence; Sydney Smith plays devil's advocate in a world of planners and worriers; Cavafy urges us to value the journey more than the destination.

All remind us that moral compasses can be set and reset at any time in our lives. Always we have the power to see life differently.

" I always knew that deep down in every human heart there was mercy and generosity. No-one is born hating another person because of the colour of his skin or his background or his religion. People must learn to hate, and, if they can learn to hate, they can be taught love, for love comes more naturally to the human heart than its opposite. "

Nelson Mandela: Long Walk To Freedom

A genuine and unequivocal power to forgive is something I find both rare and inspiring: the father of a young girl killed in the Omagh bombing extending the hand of reconciliation to the IRA: a former prisoner of the Japanese on the River Kwai embracing one of his former captors.

If you ever visit Coventry, take a walk in the Gothic space which was once the nave of the medieval cathedral and pause before the sculpture of an embrace. It's by Josefina de Vasconcellos, it's called 'Reconciliation' and it stands on the spot where, during World War II, the Luftwaffe dropped the bombs which destroyed the old cathedral as they were systematically ravaging the city of Coventry. This makes it special for me – not merely beautiful, but moving.

If there were a Mandela award for demonstrations of the power of love over hatred I would nominate the citizens of Coventry who conceived and commissioned this lovely sculpture.

Nelson

Some of our important life choices will rest upon whatever assumptions we make about people. To give or not to give? To trust or not to trust? To punish or pardon?

To make the Mandela assumption carries risks – of being seen as a soft touch, of being betrayed or exploited; but when something we say or do brings out the best in someone, the rewards can be priceless.

These words were written by a man whose faith in human nature was tested in a way few of us will ever experience.

Born and raised in a South Africa which indoctrinated all Blacks with the belief that they and their culture were inferior to the colonising Dutch and British, he had to suffer many insults at the hands of white people. As a young, proud, ambitious, qualified lawyer, he was once ordered by a white woman to carry her bags from the taxi into her hotel – a perfectly 'normal' demand in South Africa at that time. And, of course, she called him 'boy'.

A man born in the Transkei, whose family were respected rulers, he soon found himself propelled into the maelstrom of conflict and hatred that he came to describe as 'The Struggle'. It cost him not only twenty-seven years of his life in prison but appalling treatment at the hands of arrogant racists, prejudiced judges, hostile police, brutal prison officers and disloyal friends. It would be tempting to describe his treatment as 'humiliating', but you cannot humiliate a man who refuses to surrender his self-esteem.

When he came to power as President of the new South Africa, most of us would have forgiven him for lighting a few fires of retribution under the toes of those who had abused him. But what I find amazing is the total absence of bitterness and his unshakeable belief in the potential of the human heart for love and goodness.

M a n d e l a

"God is our guide! From field, from wave,
From plough, from anvil and from loom;
We come, our country's rights to save,
And speak a tyrant faction's doom:
We raise the watchword liberty,
We will, we will, we will be free!

God is our guide! No swords we draw,
We kindle not war's battle fires;
By reason, union, justice, law,
We claim the birthright of our sires
We raise the watchword liberty,
We will, we will, we will be free! "

George Loveless: Song of Liberty.

These lines are remarkable not so much for the quality of the poetry as for the power of their message. They are a reminder of the cornerstones of the civilisation we take for granted if we live in a democratic society: the right to free speech and free association, the right to protest against injustice, and the duty to do so peacefully – 'by reason, union, justice, law'.

In 1833 the farm workers believed they had a just cause; but they had also seen what happened across the Channel in France when revolutionaries turned the streets into a blood bath – and they wanted none of it.

In twenty-first century Britain these cornerstones are again under threat: from people with power who seek to limit the freedoms which brave men have fought for from Magna Carta onwards, and from those who believe that they are justified in using violence in the pursuit of their cause.

Our traditions are only as safe as the people who actively preserve them, and our institutions are only as strong as the support we give them. The price of freedom is still eternal vigilance and it is still true that for evil to succeed it only takes good men to stay silent. When a piece of our freedom dies, 'ask not for whom the bell tolls – it tolls for thee'.

And when these precious values are threatened do we stay silent?

These lines were written in prison by a farm worker whose only crime was to form the earliest known trade union. In 1833 the landowners of Dorset imposed a cut in wages on their farm workers which took them below the bread line. Six men met in a Tolpuddle cottage to found the Friendly Society of Agricultural Labourers Association.

They were convicted of treason and deported to Australia. Such was the outcry from the British public that the Government was forced to back down and repatriate them. Loveless spent some time farming in Essex on his return, before emigrating to Canada. He founded a church in Siloam and lived there until he died.

In Tolpuddle today they are commemorated by the Martyrs' Museum, founded and funded by the trades' union movement. The local pub has been renamed The Martyrs' Inn. *Its sign shows a labourer in the foreground in peasant clothes and, in the background a group dressed in the tall hats of early nineteenth century gentlemen. Beneath is the caption 'Who was then the gentleman?'*

> **"** We tried to do some faithful things …. they weren't enough – but they were something… **"**

Ted King: A Good Place to Be

Who was it who changed South Africa for ever?

We could answer that question in so many ways. An obvious one would be to focus on the major players on the political stage; on Mandela, on his colleagues in the ANC, on F W de Klerk, who finally had the wisdom to see that apartheid's game was up; on statesmen around the world who brought pressure to bear on the South African government.

But we could also put forward as candidates those many, nameless South Africans who, in their daily lives, their behaviour and attitude refused to accept the spurious hierarchy of race supremacy and embraced the common humanity of all races and skin colours.

Their 'something', even when 'not enough', added up to a powerful force for change without which the stirring words of anti-apartheid leaders would have been cries in the wilderness. Without them there would have been no battle and no victory.

Ted

I guess we would all like to make the world a better place, and, when we hear John Lennon's *Imagine*, have our own dream of what that might be for us and the people we love. Few of us can make things happen in the corridors of power. We may not be able to do 'enough' but, like Ted King, we can do 'something'.

They were momentous times: South Africa torn apart; a government ruthlessly enforcing apartheid; a black and coloured population responding with everything from silent disobedience to dramatic acts of defiance; a white population split between liberals, apartheid hard liners and all shades in between.

In the middle of all this was Ted King, Dean of St. George's, Cape Town from 1958 – 1988, and team member thereafter… A man who put his conscience, his compassion and his God before obedience to the state; a man who married couples from different races in defiance of the law, whose church became a rallying point for protest, who marched in the struggle for freedom and knew the force of water cannon, who was arrested and dumped in a police van for trying to save a demonstrator from a beating, who one day discovered a bomb strapped to his car.

Outside St. George's a notice proclaims: 'This church is open to all people at all times at all services'. Throughout his ministry, Ted King kept that promise.

In his book, A Good Place to Be, *with a modesty foreign to modern celebrity autobiographies, he makes the Cathedral the hero of his account and describes his own part in it with humility and an engaging humour. As he joined a group of black women in a march on Parliament, he comments 'I felt odd – but righteous.'*

The quotation at the head of this chapter contains the closing words of the book – entirely typical of a man who saw his own achievements in the context of the contribution of others and the needs of his country.

K i n g

> " '*Take some more tea,*' the March Hare said to Alice very earnestly. '*I've had nothing yet,*' Alice replied, in an offended tone, '*so I can't see how I can take more.*'
> '*You mean you can't take less,*' said the March Hare. '*It's very easy to take more than nothing.*' "

Lewis Carroll: Alice In Wonderland

Happiness is about expectations. If you expect nothing you cannot be disappointed, for it is impossible to have less than nothing, as the March Hare points out with impeccable logic.

But it was called the Mad Hatter's Tea Party, and to Alice it seemed reasonable to expect to be offered a cup of tea. Instead, she found a teapot into which her hosts were stuffing a dormouse and an arcane debate, worthy of an Oxford don, on whether you could have more or less than nothing.

The March Hare's verbal gymnastics did nothing to address the gap between her expectations and the reality of being without tea. And so she became unhappy.

It is usually the case with our states of discontent; it is not what we have or don't have, but the shortfall between our expectations and our realities. The marathon runner is unhappy that he can no longer run nearly twenty-seven miles in under four hours; the arthritis sufferer is delighted that he can make it to the bus stop without a wheel chair. It's all about expectations – often aggravated, as in Alice's case, by what we perceive others to have. They all had tea, Alice had none.

Expectations are energising and life-enhancing. They drive us to achieve; they provoke us to excellence and they move the levers of the world. To be without expectations is to be without hope,

Lewis

without optimism, without the prospect of a journey to a better place. But when expectations are unfulfilled and without the prospect of fulfilment, the shortfall can curdle our good nature and cause us to turn sour and sad.

There comes a time for all of us, if we are to remain sane, balanced and cheerful human beings, to accept that certain of our aspirations may never be achieved.

And when we cannot change our world, the only route to contentment may be to change our expectations.

Charles Dodgson (1812-1898) was well-known for his 'day job' as an Oxford don, writing learned works on Euclid and Symbolic Logic. His abiding fame, however, as Lewis Carroll, derives from a trip on the River Isis in a rowing boat with the young Liddell sisters. 'Tell us a story,' they pleaded. The result was Alice's Adventures in Wonderland, *created as he rowed and later honed and developed into the version that made it the most quoted English work apart from the Bible and Shakespeare.*

In 1864 he presented it to Alice; the following year, Macmillan published it, quickly selling five thousand copies. Dodgson hated the limelight and kept his Lewis Carroll identity secret from strangers. He had other talents which brought him fame apart from his writing. As a photographer he portrayed royalty and celebrities and was described as having 'a special genius for depicting little English girls that is as brilliant in its way as Alice'.

He was a prodigious letter writer – on all kinds of subjects: anti-blood sports and vivisection, electoral reform, religious tolerance (he once wrote to Ellen Terry, the actress, begging her to change the ending of Merchant of Venice *where Shylock is forced to convert to Christianity).*

Dodgson was an ingenious inventor of gadgets and puzzles, inventing, among other things, a version of Scrabble *and probably the earliest travelling chess set.*

He died of pneumonia, celibate and unmarried, in 1898. We can only wonder how different life might have been for a man who loved children, had his day job as a Christ Church don not compelled him to be ordained and remain celibate!

C a r r o l l

> " Annual income twenty pounds, annual expenditure nineteen and six, result happiness. Annual income twenty pounds, annual expenditure twenty pounds ought and six, result misery. "

Charles Dickens: Mr. Micawber in David Copperfield

Spending involves making life choices. Consciously or unconsciously what we choose to do with our money obeys some inner compass of priorities and values. This applies most obviously to the 'big' purchases: the size and location of the house we live in, the car we drive, whether we send our children to state or private schools, whether we pay for private medicine or use the NHS, how much we spend on clothes, how important it is for us to wear 'exclusive designer' as opposed to High Street chain.

If we are in 'happiness' mode, the choices we make are, by definition, affordable. But if we have drifted into 'misery' mode we can put at risk something precious in our lives, whether that be our pride, our reputation, our independence, or a relationship with another person who means something to us and is affected in some way by our failure to manage money.

The will to move from 'misery' to 'happiness' may lead us to revisit all those life choices which carry a price tag and to ask ourselves: which of these things are dispensable and which add real value to the quality of our lives?

C h a r l e s

Born in 1812, Charles Dickens was as large as any of the characters he created. When describing events in his own life he would use the language of hyperbole like the most verbose of his creations; 'no-one knows suffering like mine ...' he once wrote in a letter.

His energy in both living and writing was prodigious; his face had 'the life and soul in it of fifty human beings'. He travelled throughout the UK and Europe (twice visiting the USA) lecturing and performing. He loved enacting scenes from his novels, throwing himself into the parts with the flair and passion of an accomplished actor. But, although well-travelled, he needed 'the magic lantern of London street life ... where laughter and misery went hand in hand, where the poorest lay huddled and dying in doorways a few yards from the mansions of the rich' (Peter Ackroyd).

His family had experienced debtors' prison and it was his father from whom he first heard the words spoken in our quotation by Mr. Micawber. Dickens fought tirelessly against poverty, bad housing, bad sanitation, the death penalty (after witnessing a double hanging in Horsemonger Lane) and the injustices of Victorian society.

He met the Queen and the President of the USA and became so famous that railway companies would hold up trains for him. People queued for hours to get tickets for his performances. Despite all this, he was frequently depressed. His personal life was blighted by a marriage which became increasingly unhappy, and, throughout his life he kept falling in 'love without hope' with younger women whom he idealised and, in his writing, turned into Dora and Estella.

He died of a stroke in 1870 while in the process of writing The Mystery of Edwin Drood, *and is buried beneath the flagstones of Westminster Abbey.*

> " Oh Lord! Save me, save those I love – brothers, parents, friends, and even my enemies – from ever having to look upon a summer without flowers, a cage without birds, a hive without bees, a house without children! "

Victor Hugo

I don't know another poet who expressed more passionately than Victor Hugo a love of children. In one of his verses he says 'come on kids, invade my house and my garden, shake my floors, my ceilings, my staircases; run, buzz about the place like bees in a field. My joy and happiness will be to follow you and enjoy your youthfulness!'

Not many of us would be willing for such an invitation to be taken literally! But those of us who have children know what it is to have our hearts possessed and our lives shaped by their arrival and the continuous demands they make on us until such time as they reach that (some would say, mythical) territory known as 'off our hands'.

And for a critical period of their development they create a dynamic tension between our various life goals. Perhaps the most serious is the tug of war between our parenting role and our work/social/material ambitions.

In making life choices around child-care we are torn between a desire to spend time with them and our own needs for stimulus, challenge, income and personal growth which, up until the point when they arrived, were met in the world of work.

We are all individuals. We all have our priorities; our chosen givens. Is it a given that we are there at bedtime to read them a story? To make sure that we're there to see her Virgin Mary in the nativity play? Or his attempt to run the hundred metres at sports day? Or are our givens driven by our careers and our choice to keep up with our peers on the housing ladder? In later years, which will we most regret missing: the award ceremony where she collected first prize for music, or that sales meeting which we handled so brilliantly?

At one end of the spectrum is a City high-flier who finds the idea of putting a career on hold utterly unthinkable; at the other, a young mother who was woken up in the night by her three year old crying, not for her, but for his nanny. It upset her so much that she gave up work and became a full time mum!

Victor Hugo was born in 1802 and spent his early years with a family which accompanied his father, an officer in Napoleon's army, in his campaigns across Spain and Italy. Eventually he experienced a more settled life in the Faubourg Saint Jacques in Paris.

A young prodigy as a writer, he lied about his age and read out a poem to the Académie Française when only fifteen. He became a giant of French literature, producing novels like Les Misérables, *plays like* Hernani *and collections of poetry such as* Les Feuilles d'Automne, *published in 1830, from which this quotation is taken.*

Hugo also played an active part in French politics, becoming a member of the Republican Government post the revolution of 1848. And when Napoleon III came to power in the coup of 1851 he went into exile in Brussels, and later the Channel Isles from where he wrote angrily about the repression of liberty in France and branded the Emperor 'Napoleon Le Petit'.

In his personal life he knew the joy of children and grandchildren and the tragedy of losing both a son and a daughter.

In 1870, now back in Paris, he enlisted, at the age of sixty-eight, in the National Guard to defend the city against the Prussian army. He died in 1885, was accorded a funeral 'plus que royale' by the nation and lies with other French 'greats' in the Pantheon.

'One of the most precious jewels of the spirit of France.' (Jules Stegg)

66 The means by which we live have outdistanced the ends for which we live. Our scientific power has outrun our spiritual power. We have guided weapons and misguided men. 99

Martin Luther King: Strength To Love

Technologically precocious and morally retarded. This seems to be the nub of Martin Luther King's accusation. And he was speaking in the 1960's. Since then the pace of scientific and technical progress has accelerated beyond anything he could have imagined.

We are now in the age of the super-smart, an age in which smart is outsmarted and outdated in a matter of months. Yesterday it was smart to have a mobile phone; today you must have one that takes photographs, transmits them to other mobile phones, gets you the weather in Bangkok, the answer to some pub quiz question, plays your favourite music, tells you the time, wakes you up in the morning, allows you to send written messages, does everything, in fact, except run your bath and scratch your back. Or am I out of date already?

Amazing progress in our ability to communicate with one another, spawning a frenzy of marketing/buying which drives us – especially the young and the competitive – to own the latest, smartest, smallest, neatest, most multifunctional, most designer-sexy.

If we stop for a moment to consider what King is saying, it doesn't make the progress any less amazing; but it does move the spotlight from the means of communication to its content

M a r t i n

and purpose. What is the point of installing the latest voice recognition technology if, when your customers finally get there, your answer makes them angry?

What is the point of being able to communicate anywhere, anytime, anyplace at the speed of light with your family and friends, if all you do is make them wish you hadn't bothered? And what is the point of owning the most sophisticated long range camera if all you do with it is invade privacy to generate gossip?

Sometimes we have to choose where to invest our time and energy: will it be on means or ends, on the technology of delivery or the message itself?

In 1935, six year old King said goodbye to two close white friends because in Atlanta , Georgia, blacks and whites were not allowed to be educated together. And at his black school he began to learn, through his schoolmates, the human cost of the South's segregation laws (his own family was comfortable if not wealthy, his father being a Baptist pastor.)

As he grew to maturity three powerful forces shaped his character and destiny: his Christian faith, his passion to bring freedom and equality to America's blacks, and his commitment to the teachings and example of Mahatma Gandhi.

When Rosa Parks, in 1955, refused to give up her seat on a bus to a white woman, King soon found himself at the head of a freedom movement which commanded the world's attention. It was a campaign which saw him attacked (sometimes physically) by racist whites and militant blacks, but he remained committed to non-violence, earning him the respect of President Kennedy and statesmen around the world, and, in 1964, the Nobel Peace Prize.

At last the Federal Government intervened to ensure that legislation in all States would reflect the US Constitution's 'self-evident truth, that all men are created equal.'

He once said 'I submit to you that if a man hasn't discovered something worth dying for, he isn't fit to live'

In April 1968 he was assassinated in Memphis, Tennessee by James Earl Ray.

L u t h e r   K i n g

" A product of the untalented, sold by the unprincipled to the utterly bewildered. "

Al Capp, American cartoonist, on abstract art.

There is a Welsh saying that the harp must be played with a smile on the face or a tear in the eye – or not at all. I feel the same about all art, music, architecture and literature. I need it to move me, make me smile, cry, stir in my seat, sit up and take notice, change me in some way. In its highest form, it evokes a sense of awe in the face of talent which I could never emulate in a thousand lifetimes. I feel this awe looking at Rembrandt's *Girl at a Window*, listening to Beethoven's *Ninth Symphony*, walking around Saint Mark's Square in Venice, reading a Shakespeare sonnet.

So when I am asked to admire a cow's intestine pickled in brine or a baked bean tin suspended from a skeleton's neck or an old sofa with its springs sticking out surrounded by women's underclothes and read the adulation such things receive in the arcane world of the art critic, I understand where Al Capp is coming from.

There – I've declared my prejudice!

But my purpose in including this quotation is not to rubbish those who genuinely find abstract art as moving as I find Rembrandt, but to encourage those who would identify with the 'utterly bewildered', to make their own choices and not be bullied by experts into an affectation of admiration.

You will know instinctively what holds meaning for you, whether or not it is fashionable or whether or not you need a three year degree course in the history of art to appreciate it.

So be the boy who cries 'the Emperor has no clothes!' Believe in your own good taste! It's good because it's yours.

A l

Alfred Gerald Caplin was born in Connecticut in 1909, a descendant of a Russian Jewish family who migrated from Latvia. When he was twelve he lost his right leg in a tram accident. Later, he would use his disability to create humour and help World War II servicemen who had lost limbs.

He launched his own cartoon strip in 1934, set in Dogpatch 'an average stone age community' and populated it with memorable characters who were followed by seventy million Americans and awarded the kind of celebrity that soap characters receive today. When Daisy Mae finally caught up with Li'l Abner and married him, it made national news headlines!

He invented for the strip a Sadie Hawkins Day, when girls could propose to and marry any man they could catch. It caught the public imagination and resulted in Sadie Hawkins dances in campuses across America. Bomber pilots painted the noses of their aircraft with Li'l Abner characters. John Steinbeck once called him 'the best writer in the world' and Marshall McLuhan declared him 'the only robust satirical force in America.'

In the 1960s he became increasingly right-wing, and attacked leading players in the protest movement (so, Joan Baez became 'Joanie Phoanie' and he introduced SWINE, 'Students Wildly Indignant about Nearly Everything.'). This change of direction caused him to lose support among many of his readers.

In 1971 he pleaded guilty to 'attempted adultery' (a crime in Wisconsin) and retired from public life. He continued to publish Li'l Abner until 1977 when, sensing that the quality of the strip was deteriorating, he apologised to his readers and walked away from Dogpatch.

In 1979 his lifelong smoking habit finally caught up with him and he died, now virtually a recluse, from emphysema. The English language owes him the invention of '-nik' words (as in 'nogoodnik' and 'loverboynik') and the phrase 'double whammy'.

Capp

" A pompous woman of his acquaintance, complaining that the head waiter of a restaurant had not shown her and her husband immediately to a table, said: 'We had to tell them who we were.' Gerald, interested, enquired 'And who were you?' "

Edith Sitwell (1887–1964)

Strange things have happened to our world with the emergence of television, the Internet and other media as dominant forces in our lives. Our obsession with fame and celebrity is perhaps the most remarkable of these changes.

There was a time when the gate to fame was narrow – restricted to the well-born, the rich, the powerful and the talented. Oh, and serious criminals! In that era few of us had aspirations to celebrity and most of us were not bothered. We got on with our lives and managed not to eat our hearts out at the thought that no-one had ever heard of us.

Today, a sea-change has occurred. Young people tick the fame box as one of their prime ambitions. People of all ages queue to appear on television shows, even those which expose them to ritual humiliation. Better to appear on TV and look stupid than not to appear at all!

Individuals of little or no talent become famous and are paraded on chat shows, to be courted and flattered as if they had won a war. Guys with special craft skills become millionaires, if their skills happen to be with feet and a ball. And which of us has not been caught in that most pathetic of dining out one-upmanships – status by association with the famous? I mean, as in 'My brother-in-law buys his groceries from a shop owned by the father of Manchester United's physiotherapist'.

Celebrity and its worship is a fact of life and we're going to have to live with it. But aspiring to it is a personal choice. There are downsides and they are big. Perhaps the most serious is becoming

E   d   i   t   h

media fodder and losing that most precious of gifts: our obscurity – the ability to preserve our privacy, not having to struggle to stay sane and decent human beings.

Sylvester Stallone, a man well used to fame, is reputed to have said: 'Celebrity is like VD. Everyone wants to f**k you until they find out what they get with it.'

Edith Sitwell was born in Scarborough in 1887, the eldest of three children who became a famous literary trio – Osbert and Sacheverell being her younger brothers. 'Together they took the dullness out of literature', said Evelyn Waugh.

In her younger years Edith worked hard at being eccentric. She gave the first reading of her poem 'Façade' with her back to the audience, half hidden behind a transparent curtain and mouthing the words through a megaphone made of compressed grass. Contrast her last performance of the same work in 1962, to music composed specially for it by William Walton, to a packed Royal Festival Hall and a five minute standing ovation.

She achieved fame in her lifetime, twice visiting the USA and associating with Hollywood luminaries like Charlie Chaplin and Marilyn Monroe. Eccentric in dress and manners, she was described as 'tall, august, with pale oval face, aquiline nose, wearing long loose robes and a turban-style head-dress, her slender fingers covered in huge rings'.

Her strangely severe features fascinated a number of artists, including Wyndham Lewis and the Russian Pavel Tchelitchew with whom she had a special relationship and to whom she addressed some of her poems.

She died in 1964 in St. Thomas's Hospital, London. Her grave in Weston, Northamptonshire, is marked by a Henry Moore sculpture of a young child's hand clasping that of an old man.

Her poetry is as eccentric as herself, full of unconventional images and allusions to classical literature and the Bible. Writing about the air raids of 1940 she says:

> *Still falls the Rain*
> *Still falls the Blood from the Starved Man's wounded Side*
> *He bears in His Heart all wounds, - those of the light that died.*

Sitwell

" Let's find out what everyone is doing. And then stop everyone from doing it. "

A P Herbert (1890–1971): Ballads for Broadbrows (1930)

It could be the manifesto of a number of bosses I have worked for. It could equally be the credo of a certain kind of politician, religious leader – parent, even.

A view of life that rests on assumptions about human beings which results in a style of leadership once called 'Theory X' by the American writer Douglas McGregor. This theory, says McGregor, assumes that people who go to work try to avoid work. And, if they are flattered or bullied into working, they will certainly not carry it out in the way their boss would have them do it.

Therefore, if you are to manage them effectively, you must set up systems, procedures, rules, disciplines and punishments which ensure that they can't avoid doing it your way; and you must be eternally vigilant for slackers.

Theory Y, on the other hand, assumes that people come to work to fulfil themselves, to find satisfying challenges and achievements, to deploy their skills, to add value, to make a difference.

This theory generates a radically different leadership style. It defines leading, managing, parenting, as the creation of a stage on which the best characteristics of human beings are invited, encouraged and enabled to perform and grow.

Theory Y leaders take risks and are vulnerable to being let down. But the rewards are incalculable. A Theory X team has one brain and a hundred hands and feet. A Theory Y team switches on the power of a hundred brains. Theory X is rooted in a belief in original sin; Theory Y in a belief in the unlimited potential of human beings to create good and amazing things.

Read Douglas McGregor's *The Human Side of Enterprise*, published in 1960 but as relevant today as it ever was. Then choose: X or Y?

A   P

I'm quoting him out of context. I don't think he'd mind. He contributed satirical articles to Punch *for many years and must have done the same!*

A man of many talents and achievements, AP Herbert was educated at Winchester and New College Oxford. He joined the Royal Navy Volunteer Reserve in 1914 and fought at Gallipoli and in France.

Wounded in 1917, he was discharged on medical grounds, freeing him to follow his two concurrent careers, writer and politician. A writer of extraordinary versatility – not only Punch*, but also ballads, musicals such as* Bless the Bride *and two ground breaking novels:* The Secret Battle*, about a Gallipoli soldier's nervous breakdown and execution for cowardice, which triggered changes in the way such cases were seen and treated by the military; and* The Water Gypsies*, which raised levels of awareness about the lives of canal folk.*

As a politician, he was the independent MP for Oxford University, and campaigned ceaselessly for the causes he cared about. These included the reform of divorce laws. In 1936/37, he steered the Matrimonial Causes Act through the Commons, allowing, for the first time, divorce on grounds of desertion, cruelty and insanity.

He passionately (and successfully) opposed the introduction of purchase tax on books. In 1945 he was listed in Winston Churchill's honours list and became Sir Alan Patrick Herbert. A painting of him by Ruskin Spear in the National Portrait Gallery shows him in old age, somewhat world weary, shabbily dressed, with eyes betraying nothing of the sparkling intellect which had created so much, or the passion which had changed the world for good. He died in 1971 in the house in Hammersmith Terrace in which he had lived for fifty-four years.

Next time you hear the song Girls Were Made To Love And Kiss *thank APH – he wrote the lyric.*

" Where there is a will to convict, there is evidence. "

Chinese proverb quoted by Jung Chang, Wild Swans (1992)

In one of my earliest jobs my boss was Bert, a man who had worked his way up through the ranks from apprentice fitter to senior manager. In this role he was responsible for recruiting the company's graduate intake. An odd choice for this position, he cherished a cluster of ingrained beliefs about universities and their issue which he took pleasure in sharing with each successive intake. Graduates, said Bert, were, virtually by definition, work-shy, impractical, prone to lateness and dubious moral behaviour – and, worst of all, socialists. It has to be said that, granted the strength of his will to convict, in any group of twenty new recruits, there would be evidence!

Bert's game is played out every day. When it's played by heads of state, it often results in a nation going to war, and, in consequence people die, lose their homes, have their lives destroyed.

When it's played by the media, the outcome doesn't appear so drastic, but can be ruinous for the lives of its victims. Once they have developed the will to convict, it is only a matter of time before the 'evidence' is published and, more often than not, backed up with pictures. Should he be grieving for some disaster? Find a picture of him smiling with a drink in his hand. Should she be showing some gravitas? Find one of her acting the clown, even if it was taken at a hen party, years ago.

It's an unfair world! Most of us would plead guilty to convicting without evidence in the court of our personal judgements on people we know, and on celebrities we don't know. The result is unlikely to be as dramatic or cruel as in the case of Jung Chang's father, but can be devastating for those who end up with ruined reputations.

Who steals my purse steals trash, 'tis something, nothing
'Twas mine, 'tis his and has been slave to thousands
But he that filches from me my good name
Robs me of that which not enriches him
And makes me poor indeed.   *Shakespeare:* Othello.

The author of two books which opened up twentieth century China to the world to an astonishing and unprecedented degree. She was born in Sichuan Province, China in 1952. Hers was an affluent childhood during which her parents, both senior officials in the Communist Party, enjoyed the privileges of the ruling elite. They had become committed Party members in the sane years of its rule, when it brought a fairness and concern for the poor which China had never known under the warlords, the Japanese invaders or the Kuomintang.

Soon, however, under Mao Zedong, things changed. Chang joined the Red Guards as a teenager and at first supported the Cultural Revolution, but was appalled by the violent attacks on teachers, intellectuals and Party officials. She saw her father targeted and his reputation, his sanity and finally his life destroyed, causing her to lose belief in Mao.

She tells how she feigned grief for Mao's death, adding: 'weeping for Mao was, perhaps, just another programmed act in their programmed lives'. In post-Cultural Revolution China she obtained a degree in English in the re-opened University of Sichuan and taught there for a while. Then, in 1978, she left for the UK, gained a PhD at York University and, later, lectured at the London School of Oriental and African Studies. In the 1990s she retired to write her books – Wild Swans *(1992) and* Mao: The Unknown Story *(2005).*

She married a British historian, Jon Halliday, who became her co-author for the book on Mao. The couple live in West London. Chang frequently visits her family and friends in China. It is her greatest wish that, one day soon, the ban on her books there will be lifted to allow a thousand million Chinese to read this account of their history.

One contributor to the Internet reviews of Wild Swans *wrote: 'a book that made me both deeply ashamed and proud to be a human being, often on the same page'.*

C h a n g

" Happy are those who lose imagination:
They have enough to carry with ammunition.
Their spirit drags no pack.
Their old wounds, save with cold, can no more ache.
Having seen all things red,
Their eyes are rid
Of the hurt of the colour of blood for ever.
And terror's first constriction over,
Their hearts remain small-drawn.
Their senses in some scorching cautery of battle
Now long since ironed,
Can laugh among the dying, unconcerned. "

Wilfred Owen: Insensibility

Few people in the Western world have had firsthand experience of war. For most of us it is relayed second hand via our TV sets, cinema screens and the accounts we read in the press. So it is difficult for us to relate to the pain and the passion which drove Owen to write these words.

He is writing about a hidden casualty of war. He is writing about the death of human sensitivity which occurs when we send our young people into battle and make them kill other human beings.

Wilfred

Their hearts become 'small drawn' their senses 'cauterised' in the heat of conflict so that they 'can laugh among the dying unconcerned'.

I have seen this happen to colleagues of mine during my service in the forces. Some piece of their humanity dies in the process of killing. You hope that it will live again when the killing stops, but you know that for some it is a permanent death, that their hearts and minds are scarred forever.

When we choose, by word or vote, to support war, how many of us weigh in the balances of argument this hidden cost? What price should we put on the death of a piece of our humanity?

Wilfred Owen, for me the most powerful and passionate of the war poets, was born in 1893. Before setting eyes on a dead body he wrote patriotic verses like:

> *'O meet it is and passing sweet*
> *To live in peace with others*
> *But sweeter still and far more meet*
> *To die in war for brothers.'*

Wilfred joined the Manchester Regiment in France at the end of 1916 and fought in the horror that was the Somme. Soon he was writing: 'unburiable bodies, the most execrable sights on earth. In poetry we call them glorious.'

Later, in 1917, he was suspected of being on the verge of a nervous breakdown and sent to Craiglockhart Hospital where he met Siegfried Sassoon. Sassoon opened up for him the literary world of London and effectively launched him as a poet. He was discharged from Craiglockhart and in 1918 rejoined his regiment at the front. On November 4th he was leading his men in an attempt to cross the Sambre et Oise canal when he was shot dead by a German marksman. One week later the Armistice which ended World War I was signed. He is buried in the village cemetery at Ors, on the canal he died trying to cross.

" 25 December 1914: Two hours later we passed through Zillebeke. A skeleton village where not a single house – not one – remained standing. Everything is in ruins: the church, its belfry, the cross in the cemetery. We'll find no shelter here! Midnight. We file silently into the trench. The Germans in the opposite trenches are singing a Christmas carol punctuated by the sound of gunfire. Poor little God of love, born this night, how did you ever manage to love mankind? "

Maurice Laurentin: Carnet d'un Fantassin

These words appear in a selection of writers' reflections on World War I. I discovered them in a Flanders' battlefield museum after spending four days tracking the activities of my father's battalion and visiting the killing fields which saw the slaughter of four million young men. In my mind I linked them to a remarkable piece of film kept constantly running in one of the museums.

The film surveys the now green and pleasant land over which the armies fought so ferociously, from the vantage point of a hot air balloon. A powerful commentary bade us look down at the now tranquil scene of our quarrel, remember our common humanity and question whether the barbarity that was World War I could ever be justified before a court of civilised people.

Maurice

With these poignant words, Laurentin is forcing us to face the same question; he is not shaking his fist in anger but his head in sorrow. Is mankind, which somehow the little God of love managed to love, capable of learning from past eras of shame and holding back the dogs of war while pursuing more civilised and intelligent means of resolving conflict? On a personal level, there are times when we are faced with a choice: the pursuit of a quarrel versus the pursuit of reconciliation.

Before making that choice it might help if we climbed into our hot air balloon, soared a few thousand feet, looked down at the ground staked out for the duel – and realised how small our quarrel looks from a place a little nearer heaven. And, if we make the right choice, who knows, the little God of love might find us just a wee bit more lovable.

Maurice Laurentin was born in 1886 and graduated as an architect in 1914. He joined the French Army as an infantry officer and spent the whole of the war at the front.

'Four years of his life, out in the open, without shelter, exposed to water, mud, ice, scorching sun, hunger and rotting corpses; four years of assaults, gas, mines, bombardments … How can a man who never forgot what life was all about put his life at such continuous risk?' Even in the heat of battle he never lost his human sensitivity.

His diary is among the most compelling and compassionate ever written and his pencil drawings from the trenches are skilful and moving. In 1939 he went to war again and found himself a prisoner of war in Belgium. As the others were being marched off by the Feldwebel commander he slid out of the ranks and hid behind a wall… and when they had all gone, went home!

A Latin scholar (he once translated Virgil) he uttered his last words in that language in 1959.

L a u r e n t i n

"
O fat white woman whom nobody loves,
Why do you walk through the fields in gloves,
When the grass is soft as the breast of doves
And shivering sweet to touch?
O why do you walk through the fields in gloves,
Missing so much and so much?
"

Frances Cornford: To a Fat Woman Seen from a Train (1910)

I once shook hands with Diana Princess of Wales. She wore gloves. They were a fashion accessory; but they also made a statement about the formality of the occasion, about the absence of any personal meaning which hands touching hands can convey.

I watched her on television reaching over a bed to touch the hands of an AIDS victim. She wore no gloves, and the touch of her bare hands on his sent a message to the watching world: 'He's a human being too – and it's OK to touch him.'

Gloves in warm weather: a symbolic announcement of formality, protecting a handshake from any misconception as to its meaning. And in the poem, a device to protect our fat white lady from a close encounter with nature. For her, gloves are the adoption of a wary, keep-your-distance approach to life's great possibilities, guarding the hand from the threat of stinging nettles whilst depriving her of the sublime sensation of grass 'softer than the breast of doves'.

F r a n c e s

Some of us go through life wearing gloves – a kind of spiritual glove which protects us from the risks and turbulence of close encounters with other human beings, whilst depriving us of their richness and enormous potential for happiness.

We don't arrive in the world wearing gloves – they have to be put on. And if they can be put on, they can also be taken off.

'God, I can push the grass apart, And lay my finger on Thy heart'. I think the American poet, Edna St. Vincent Millay, probably wrote these words with the gloves off.

Frances Cornford was born in Cambridge in 1886 and lived all her life in its academic ambience. Her grandfather was Charles Darwin and her husband, Francis, a Fellow of Trinity College. Their home was a meeting place for artists and writers and their circle included Bertrand Russell, Rupert Brook and Virginia Woolf.

Her first poems were published in 1910. By 1954 she had become the 'official choice' of the Poetry Book Society and in 1959 she was awarded the Queen's Medal for Poetry. A competent linguist, she translated works from both French and Russian.

Her Fat Woman *poem had the distinction of being parodied by, first G K Chesterton and later, A E Housman, and some of today's critics, perhaps overlooking the fact that it was written in Edwardian England, make a point of commenting on its lack of political correctness!*

A drawing of her by Sir William Rothenstein shows refined, handsome features with elegant bone structure, gentle eyes and sensuous lips. Contemporaries described her as striking, attractive, gentle, and friendly; a person of great warmth and amusing conversation who had an endearing capacity for mislaying her possessions. Hard to believe that she harboured any malice towards the woman glimpsed from the train!

She died of heart failure in 1960 and is buried in Saint Giles cemetery, Cambridge.

" Take short views of life: never further than dinner or tea. "

Rev. Sydney Smith

When I first read this exhortation I had passed my sixtieth birthday and crossed the threshold into the twilight zone of the Third Age.

The Third Age: when, for the first time in your life, you believe in your own mortality; when your annual medical confirms that, were you a car, you would be well advised to trade you in. And I had realised that what made me happy or miserable, buoyant or depressed, energised or listless, excited or bored with life was not the actuality of my life but how I perceived it.

The key lay not so much in my condition but in my self-talk – the myriad messages I am processing in my mind by the minute. This 'law' of self-talk allows a millionaire, with every material thing he ever wanted, to be miserable to the point of suicide and a hard-up student nurse to be happy and fulfilled.

It explains why some disabled people, with every reason to complain about the hand that life has dealt them, are capable of communicating cheerfulness and lifting your spirit. It explains why, for some of us glasses will be for ever half-full, while, for others they will be half empty.

S y d n e y

For me, Smith's words are saying: 'Look, you have a choice. You can either fill your waking thoughts with the gloom of approaching winter and savour, in advance, its dank coldness. Or you can enjoy today's sunshine; go where the music and laughter of life can be found and top up your reservoir of joy.'

There are times in all our lives when the right decision is to 'seize the day' and leave to whichever God we believe in, the uncontrollable vagaries of the future.

Rev. Sydney Smith was born in Woodford in 1771. He attended Winchester College and New College, Oxford and despised the education at both. He was no institution's favourite son, yet became Prebendary of Bristol cathedral and Dean of St. Paul's.

It was not until sixty-four years after his death, in 1845, that a plaque in his honour was unveiled in Bristol cathedral: 'A tardy recognition of one who reasoned liberally, illuminating civic wisdom with Christian charity, and political judgement with social wit, and common sense with uncommon insight.'

Smith was ahead of his time as champion of the abolition of child labour, equal status for Catholics, and women's rights. But he was chiefly famous for being a larger-than-life character in every sense. Portraits and cartoons of him show us a man who has enjoyed good dinners! A man of intelligence, breadth of tolerance, warmth, humour and wit; a man who treated his servants in much the same way as he treated Prime Ministers.

His lectures at the Royal Institution, Albemarle Street, were so popular they caused traffic jams of horse-driven carriages. He once said: 'I never read a book before reviewing it – it prejudices a man so.'

Smith

“ For my part, I travel not to go anywhere, but to go. I travel for travel's sake. The great affair is to move; to feel the needs and hitches of our life more nearly; to come down off this feather bed of civilisation, and find the globe granite underfoot all strewn with cutting flints.

Alas, as we get up in life, and are more preoccupied with our affairs, even a holiday is a thing that must be worked for. To hold a pack upon a pack-saddle against a gale out of the freezing north is no high industry, but it is one that serves to occupy and compose the mind. And when the present is so exacting, who can annoy himself about the future? ”

Robert Louis Stevenson: Travels with a Donkey in the Cévennes

This, it seems to me, is all about concentrating on the task in hand and living in the 'now'. Stevenson was doing just that as he held a pack upon the pack saddle when a 'Hooley' was blowing out of the north. He was concentrating on the immediate physical task at hand, but I believe that we can take a psychological view of this as well.

It's a fact that the mind can't hold more than one thought at a time – we may think it can and I knew of an old lady who reckoned that she could knit, watch TV, have a conversation and still plan her next meal all at the same time. Trying to hold more than one thought in mind at a time is even more impossible than trying to do two things at once.

But, we do have the ability to change our thinking patterns – no one said it would be easy but many will attest that it is possible. St Paul spoke about being "transformed by the renewing of your mind".

Whatever else he might have been, he was no mean psychologist, and those few words harbour a rich seam of insights.

It's helpful to remember this when useless emotions such as remorse or guilt engulf us – both are physically, psychologically and spiritually damaging. They pervade our memories and contaminate any lighter moments. I know, I've been there. It takes a bit of will power to catch these negative and self-defeating thoughts and push a new, more constructive thought, or activity, in place of them – but it can be done. I believe this is where we, like Stevenson, hold the pack on the pack saddle against a cold north wind. It might not be any high industry, but it concentrates and occupies the mind wonderfully and after a short while we'll find the negative stuff dissipating as life begins to look better.

You'll be so 'in the now' that the past will fade and the future will take care of itself.

So, if you're looking up at the sky from the bottom of a well, it's good to remember that climbing out starts with a first step. And the first step is to start overlaying those thoughts that are keeping you where you don't want to be, with ones that will help you get to where you want to go.

How about it?

GK Chesterton wrote of him as an author who 'seemed to pick the right word up on the point of his pen'. A Scottish born novelist, essayist, poet and travel writer, Stevenson wrote some of the great adventure stories in the English language – Treasure Island *and* Kidnapped *to name just two.*

Born in Edinburgh in 1850 he studied engineering and then law at university before recognizing that his real talents lay in writing; Chesterton's words sum up his writing style beautifully.

Never the most healthy of people, Stevenson suffered from tuberculosis and travelled widely in his search for a more healthful climate. His travel writing has given us delightful books such as Travels with a Donkey in the Cévennes *(from where the above quotation comes) and* An Inland Voyage*.*

His travels took him through America and into the South Pacific to Samoa where he finally settled with his wife Frances in 1889. Five years later he suffered what was probably a brain haemorrhage whilst living on his estate on the island of Upolo. He was 44. He is buried at the foot of a local mountain and the last two lines of his epitaph read 'Home is the sailor, home from sea, And the hunter home from the hill.'

" Setting out on the voyage to Ithaka
You must pray that the way be long,
Full of adventures and experiences.

You must always have Ithaka in your mind,
Arrival there is your predestination.
But do not hurry the journey at all.
Better that it should last many years;
Be quite old when you anchor at the island,
Rich with all you have gained on the way,
Not expecting Ithaka to give you riches.
Ithaka has given you your lovely journey.
Without Ithaka you would not have set out.
Ithaka has no more to give you now. "

C P Cavafy: Ithaka

C P

This is a metaphysical work. Its quiet message is that what we carry with us in our hearts and minds we eventually arrive at. We do not need to meet with bellicosity, brutality and anger if we refuse to carry these emotions in our hearts. What we dwell upon is very much inclined to become our experience.

We should expect our voyage (or our life) to be long with many sunny, summer mornings, the serendipity of harbours never seen before, and good, wonderful experiences, and kindnesses, and gifts, and always learning more and more.

We cannot escape our final landfall and we should arrive at its shores rich with all that we have gained along the way. We shouldn't expect anything more – all of the riches that life has offered us have been given to us during the journey to our personal Ithaka.

And yet the quality of our experiences in life and the sense of wonder and gratitude engendered during our travels will carry us on, through our beaching on Ithaka, to the new horizon that awaits us on the other side of the island, out of sight to us at the moment.

And then it will be an even better journey that we start out on.

Constantine Cavafy was born in Alexandria, Egypt, in 1863 to Greek parents. Although in his youth he lived in England, France and Constantinople before returning to Alexandria for good, he remained proudly Greek and all his poetry was written in his native language. His poems were out of kilter with contemporary Greek poetry and it was not until after his death that they achieved the acclaim they enjoy today.

From the 1950s onwards his collected works have been published several times, with tributes from such literary giants as W H Auden, Gore Vidal and Seamus Heaney. He wrote Ithaka *in 1911.*

On 29th April, 1933, aged seventy, he died of cancer of the larynx.

He left us a legacy of poetry which today is included in the curriculum in Greek schools and in universities around the world, and has a fascination for readers well beyond the boundaries of literature students.

C a v a f y

> " Books are the carriers of civilisation. Without books, history is silent, literature dumb, science crippled, thought and speculation at a standstill. Without books, civilisation would have been impossible. They are engines of change, windows on the world, 'lighthouses', as a poet said, 'erected in the sea of time". They are companions, teachers, magicians, and bankers of the treasures of the mind. Books are humanity in print. "

Barbara Tuchman

Grandfatherly advice on how to treat a book came thick and fast: 'Never turn the corners down as a bookmark, don't eat whilst reading a book; don't write in a book (took me a long time to break that habit!); and one I never understood: 'Never lend a book to a dog.'

My primary school teacher was not one of life's great motivators but, unbeknownst to her, she helped to fan the flames of my passion for books and the written word. It happened like this. To mark the 1953 Coronation, she decided that all her charges should tell her what they wanted to be when they left school. I wanted to be a lumberjack. I wanted to join the ranks of brawny, tartan-shirted, bearded men rolling massive tree trunks down British Columbian rivers.

My father's friend from the Forestry Commission suggested that I become a Forestry Officer. I would have to go to university and study one of the sciences. I didn't even know what science was, let alone a university, but it sounded good.

As I told the class that I wanted to be a Forestry Officer but that first I had to go to university, my teacher put her hands on her ample hips and laughed. 'No,' she said, 'not you, you're not bright enough.' See, I told you she was a motivator! But somewhere between that nifty bit of career guidance and my walk home from school, I reasoned that not going to university wouldn't bar me from reading. From that point, books became my unfailing companions and I read, and I read, and I still do.

Telling this story some forty years later, my best friend goaded me 'That old story again? When are you going to dump that old bag?' He had a point and I became a student with the Open University and

B a r b a r a

a wonderful new world opened up for me. I studied Greek and Roman history and literature along with the arts and humanities and I almost passed out with happiness when I received Distinctions in my examinations. My teacher turned out to be a motivator after all.

Books are indeed wonderful things and Tuchman's words show the value of them beautifully. But, before I get too carried away or serious about them, I'd like to mention a quote from Groucho Marx that I saw on a Waterstone's carrier bag: 'Outside of a dog, a book is a man's best friend. Inside of a dog it's too dark to read.'

Yes that makes for a good balance! Never lend a book to a dog, and while you're about it don't listen to your primary school teacher either!

Born in New York in 1912, Barbara Tuchman became an author, journalist and historian whose subjects covered the sweep of western civilisation from the Trojan Wars through to the American experience in Vietnam.

For a time she was the American correspondent of the New Statesman *in London, and it was as a journalist that she was able to mock those in her own profession who enjoyed terrifying and depressing their readers: 'After absorbing the news of today, one expects to find a world consisting entirely of strikes, crimes, power failures, broken water mains, stalled trains, school shutdowns, muggers, drug addicts, neo-Nazis and rapists.'*

Later she became a serious historian, winning the Pulitzer Prize twice, once for The Guns of August, *a searching analysis of the military decisions leading to the beginning of WWI, and later for* Stilwell and the American Experience in China. *The former so impressed John F Kennedy that he made it recommended reading for his staff during the Cuban missile crisis in 1962.*

Tuchman was a passionate believer in the power of history to inform and teach today's world leaders. In 1980 she reached the peak of her career as a Lecturer, when she was asked by the US government to deliver the Jefferson Lecture.

Her writing is characterised by an ability to say a lot in a short, pithy sentence, as in: 'Every successful revolution puts on, in time, the robes of the tyrant it has deposed.'

She died in Greenwich, Connecticut in 1989.

T u c h m a n

Endings

Five very different takes on approaching life's twilight zone. The author of Ecclesiastes bids us accept the ending of things gracefully; Aunt Hannah bids us farewell disgracefully and sends a stab wound of guilt into all of us who have patronised and disrespected the elderly; Grayson and Coward are warmed by memories of special times with special people; and Tagore asks us to see death, not as an end, but as a transition.

The five together remind us that, while we have no control over the ending of our lives, we have many choices in the way we perceive it and approach it. Do we refuse to think about it and let it surprise us like a mugger in a dark alley? Do we 'rage against the dying of the light'? Do we accept it with stoic resignation and get down to the practicalities of writing our will? Or do we embrace it as a passage to another and better world?

We always have a choice. It is possible to see even death differently.

" To everything there is a season, and a time for every purpose under heaven: a time to be born and a time to die; a time to plant and a time to pluck up ……. a time to break down and a time to build up …. a time to mourn and a time to dance ….. a time to embrace and a time to refrain from embracing ….. a time to keep silence and a time to speak… "

Ecclesiastes 3 verses 1 – 7: The Bible

A time for everything: and a time for the ending of everything. Something which was part of our lives – someone, perhaps – is no longer there and we are left with a painful void. A job; a career; life in a special place; a relationship; a role we had in someone's life; a special person.

And we start the Grieving Journey. At first, disbelief, denial, anger even – 'it can't be happening'. Then acceptance and, with acceptance, pain and depression – 'it has happened and life will never be the same'.

At this stage of the Journey we wallow, our faces are turned towards the past, on what has been, on what we have lost. In some cases we lose the energy to live our normal lives and have to drag ourselves to do things which were a normal part of our daily lives.

Thankfully, most of us find the will and the resources within ourselves to move on to the third stage: the rebuilding and reshaping of our lives, finding ways of coping with the loss, and the rediscovery of optimism – 'life goes on and I can and will get back in control of mine'.

Slowly we turn about and face the future once more and we dare to believe that life is worth living. What we have lost becomes repositioned in our memory, and we learn to reclaim in our reminiscences the good times.

Two things about this Journey. First, we all go through it in our own unique way and to our own timetable – no-one can organise it for us or tell us how or when we should be travelling any part of it. Secondly, whereas the loss is usually out of our control, how we travel the Grieving Road is very much up to us. We can, if we wish, choose to stay stuck.

The opening words of Ecclesiastes, 'The words of the Preacher, the son of David, king in Jerusalem' seem to proclaim that the author was the legendary King Solomon.

But many modern scholars dispute this and point to linguistic and other evidence that it was written much later than the reign of Solomon (970 – 930 BC), probably in the third century BC. So, we don't really know who wrote these words.

There must, however have been powerful reasons why they were attributed to the famous King of Israel; who so fascinated the Queen of Sheba; who built a temple to the specifications of his God, which became one of the wonders of his world; and whose legendary wisdom spawned anecdotes like his famous resolution of the dispute of two mothers who claimed the same baby. ('Cut the babe in two and let them have half each', whereupon one of them said: 'Let her have him,' confirming her claim to be the real mother.)

Solomon was a man of peace, who led a new age of rebuilding after years of conflict under his father David had established Israel's security and preserved their national identity.

A much more colourful character than some anonymous scholar in the third century BC. So, although the ethos of Ecclesiastes as a whole seems a bit gloomy for a man who lived a life of optimism and achievement and although he probably didn't write these words, somehow I wish he had!

Ecclesiastes

" Piss off. "

Hannah Houlton

A translation of this 'Piss off' would be: Excuse me, but I think you're mistaking me for somebody else. You probably think of me as this feeble old bag of bones scrunched up in a corner of her bed. You couldn't be more wrong.

At eighteen I won a beauty contest – ask my niece to show you my photo and take a look at the gorgeous brown eyes and the thick dark hair with its autumn tints. I am the wife of Jim Houlton. Together we managed pubs for Bents Brewery on Merseyside – tough pubs in the dockland area of Scotland Road, and posh pubs in the leafy suburbs of Allerton.

When Jim was called up in the RAF in World War II, and Liverpool was being bombed by the Luftwaffe, I ran the dockland pub on my own; I stopped fights, threw out drunks, changed barrels, served good beer, sacked thieving bar staff and managed the accounts.

I left school at thirteen but taught myself all I needed to know and some of the things I wanted to – like playing the piano. I never read a note of music but I could accompany any sing-a-long at any party. When I was around, people seemed to want to sing. And, somehow, I made them laugh. I could swear like any docker but in some funny, quirky way they treated me like a family treasure.

So stop waking me when I choose to sleep. Stop putting me to bed when I want to stay awake. Stop rationing my whisky. And don't tut when you discover a dram smuggled into my handbag by a kind relative. Stop talking to me as if I were some educationally sub-normal child.

Look beyond and beneath what you see, and talk to the person I have been and still am. Above all, respect my wish to stay in control of what remains of my life.

Aunt

She was ninety-seven and lay dying. My sisters had already made tentative funeral arrangements. We stood at the foot of her bed in the old people's home in Liverpool, while two carers with big hearts and seriously Scouse accents tried to rouse her. I saw an untidy bundle of bedclothes and, sticking out of its top end, a tousled ball of white hair.

She had rolled herself into a foetal position and I marvelled at how tiny a space this human being, whom we had known all our lives, now seemed to need. The carers shook her gently and spoke to her in the way carers do when they spend their lives communicating with people who are losing their brain cells.

'Hannah! Your nieces are here. Your nephew's here – he's come all the way from Winchester to see you. Aren't you going to say hello to them?'

The little bundle stirred and the head lifted ever so slightly – just enough to free the mouth and open one eye. She said 'Piss off!' And they were the last words I heard her speak.

Hannah

"When I have fears, as Keats had fears,
Of the moment I'll cease to be
I console myself with vanished years
Remembered laughter, remembered tears,
And the peace of the rolling sea.

When I feel sad, as Keats felt sad,
That my life is nearly done
It gives me comfort to dwell upon
Remembered friends who are dead and gone,
And the jokes we had and the fun.

How happy they are I cannot know,
But happy am I who loved them so. "

Noel Coward

N o e l

This book is largely about life choices. So what is a poem about death doing here? Death is the one certainty we must face and a reality over which we don't have choices.

But what Noel Coward's lovely words show us is that there is an infinity of ways in which we may look at death, a huge range of choices in the way we approach it, talk about it, prepare for it. If we are blessed with belief in an afterlife, death becomes merely a threshold to be crossed: 'When I tread the verge of Jordan . . . . . . land me safe on Canaan's side.'

But what if we're among those who believe that death is literally the end? What if, for us, the realm beyond the grave is some vast unknown territory where hope is possible but certainty excluded? Has the world for us been merely a stage on which we have been no more than actors in a play of no consequence?

Coward's poem celebrates the lives of friends which were rich in laughter, friendship, love and the sharing of precious experiences; lives worthwhile for their own intrinsic quality; lives which leave beautiful footprints in the sands of time.

To keep on leaving such footprints so long as we can breathe, is not a bad way of approaching our own departure, whether or not there is a shore on the other side.

Noel Coward was born in 1889, the son of a piano salesman and an ambitious mother. It was she who encouraged his theatrical talent and he was only eighteen when he wrote his first play. He soon discovered the light touch and wit which was to make him famous with such plays as Hay Fever, Private Lives *and* Blithe Spirit. *During World War II he wrote patriotic scripts like* This Happy Breed *and the screenplay for* Brief Encounter.

Out of favour as a playwright in the immediate post-war years he became a successful cabaret performer at London's Café de Paris. In the 1960s, however, a revival of Private Lives *rekindled his popularity which, subsequently, proved to be durable.*

He was knighted in 1970 and died in Jamaica in 1973.

We owe him songs of abiding appeal like Mad Dogs And Englishmen Go Out In The Midday Sun, *and a host of memorable one-liners such as 'wit ought to be a glorious treat, like caviar; never spread around like marmalade' and 'certain women should be struck regularly, like gongs.'*

C o w a r d

" I was not aware of the moment when I first crossed the threshold of this life. What was the power that made me open out into this vast mystery like a bud in the forest at midnight? When in the morning I looked upon the light, I felt in a moment that I was no stranger in this world, that the inscrutable without name and form had taken me in its arms in the form of my own mother. Even so, in death the same unknown will appear as ever known to me. And, because I love this life, I know I shall love death as well. The child cries out when from the right breast the mother takes it away, in the very next moment to find in the left one its consolation. "

Rabindranath Tagore

An answer to the great unknown. What happens when our life comes to an end? Is it the end, darkness, eternal darkness? Is there an opening to another more beautiful world, where all reality rushes to meet us and we know that this is where we belong? With the exception of the Resurrection of Jesus, no one has ever come back to tell us. If we don't believe him then we remain in the dark.

Yet in these words of Tagore there is comfort to be found when thoughts travel to the land of 'Is that all there is?'

We don't have any idea of what it was like or when it was that we first crossed the threshold into the present life. We do know that light and loving arms welcomed us — Tagore calls it the great inscrutable in the form of his mother.

Similarly, when we die and we move from this experience into a new one we will find arms waiting for us. Why shouldn't this be? Plenty of 'last words' have been uttered that talk of joy, and peace and light — as well as the odd profanity regarding Bognor.

R a b i n d r a n a t h

108

The simplicity of the picture of the child crying out when its mother takes it from the right breast, only to find its contentment immediately in the left one, is one that brings comfort.

It's in keeping with the picture of the sailing ship moving towards the horizon, watched by grieving people; it suddenly disappears from their sight, only to be welcomed by others on another shore, who shout joyously at the ship's impending arrival.

In the end, it's all about trust.

Tagore, born in 1861 into Bengal's most distinguished dynasty, became his country's cultural giant and carved out for himself a global persona. By the time Epstein sculpted him with his long flowing locks and beard, he 'was conducted about like a holy man – not expected to carry money'.

As a writer his output was prodigious: novels, plays, short stories, poems, essays – and over two thousand songs, including the Indian and Bengali national anthems.

Some of his early education was in Brighton and University College London, but he left without a degree to pursue a life as a Bengali aristocrat, writer and global philosopher. His relations with the British were always ambivalent. On the one hand, he admired their civilisation and culture and certain special friendships with, for example, William Rothenstein, through whom he met and impressed W B Yeats. On the other, he was angered at their imperialism and tendency to do awful things to his people. He sent his knighthood back in 1919 in protest at the Amritsar massacre.

'I, for my part, wish to stand … by the side of those my countrymen who, for their so-called insignificance, are liable to suffer a degradation not fit for human beings.'

At Santiniketan, near his family home, he founded a school and university for which he toured the world to raise funds. He opposed learning by rote and championed the development of the human spirit. As early as 1893 he warned the Indian National Congress not to neglect the cause of Hindu-Muslim unity. He experienced deep personal grief, marrying a girl of ten and losing her and two of their five children while still in their youth. He died in the family home, after a long illness, in 1941. Gandhi called him ' the Great Sentinel of Indian civilisation'.

Tagore

" I do not know, truly, what we are here for upon this wonderful and beautiful earth, this incalculably interesting earth, unless it is to crowd into a few short years – when all is said, terribly short years! – every possible fine experience and adventure; unless it is to live our lives to the uttermost; unless it is to seize upon every fresh impression, develop every latent capacity; to grow as much as ever we have in our power to grow. What else can there be? If there is no life beyond this one, we have lived here to the uttermost. We've had what we've had! But if there is more life, and still more life, beyond this one, and above and under this one, and around and through this one, we shall be well prepared for that, whatever it may be. "

David Grayson

These words call us to make the most of every moment and not put our dreams and aspirations on hold or postpone our lives.

John was a hard-bitten senior manager, and he was doing work that he didn't enjoy. It showed and eventually he decided to spend some time reviewing his career and getting some pointers for his next step. At some point I asked him what his personal dream was. He wasn't used to people asking him "woolly, new-agey questions". His eyes did soften (just a bit!) and he said that he'd always wanted to travel across Canada.

D a v i d

Career coaches can be annoying; they ask questions the other person doesn't really want to hear. Questions like: "When are you going to do it then?"

He looked straight at me: "When I retire."

"Er, can you show me the piece of paper that guarantees that you'll get to retire?"

He grinned wryly; of course he couldn't.

The conversation made him think for a while, but it didn't galvanise him into action. He's still plodding towards retirement in a job that he doesn't like. Maybe he'll get to Canada - maybe he won't. He's not really coming close to living out the philosophy behind David Grayson's words.

Our lives are precious; every day that goes by inexorably brings us closer to the end of our time on this beautiful blue planet. Every action we take (even simple things like sipping from a cup of tea, or reading a page of a newspaper) brings us closer to that time.

Think about that for a second or two; it's a powerful message and it brings the reality of how we spend our time into a very sharp focus. We can't change any part of our past life; all we can do is work on the present moment and, in doing so, we can affect our future. Maybe it's not too late.

How about you? Is there something you've dreamt of doing, but have never really found the time to do?

Don't waste any more time - go and do it.

Now here's someone who was a bit of a Jekyll and Hyde character. David Grayson is the pseudonym of Ray Stannard Baker, who was born in 1870 in Michigan. At work he was well-known as a 'muck-raking' journalist (he wrote for McClure's Magazine, *and became editor of the* American Magazine, *following his part in a buy-out of it).*

Yet, once away from that life, he lived on his farm and, as David Grayson, wrote some tender and gentle books most of which dealt with the simple life and the value of friendship. He was a home-spun philosopher and deep thinker about the values of the human condition.

President Woodrow Wilson, for whom Baker worked as a press secretary in France, nominated Baker as his official biographer – and in 1940 he was awarded the Pulitzer Prize for biography.

A heart attack carried him away in the summer of 1946.

G r a y s o n

and .... finally

> " This above all: to thine own self be true,
>   And it must follow, as the night the day,
>   Thou canst not then be false to any man. "

> *William Shakespeare*: Hamlet

Who could disagree with these words of Shakespeare or fail to be stirred by them? Yet last week a politician went on television to say something he didn't believe; a football striker went down in the penalty area without a member of the opposition laying a foot on him; a young girl went to a party wearing an outfit her body was simply not designed for; a boy got involved in a gang attack on a passer-by he had never met in his life, putting him in hospital; a bride went through with a marriage ceremony despite knowing that she did not love the groom; a student started a course she knew she would hate, because her parents had persuaded her it would lead to a career they approved of; a man continued to keep his sexuality hidden from people who love him; and a salesman sold a vulnerable customer a product he knew was wrong for her in order to meet his sales target.

William

What stopped them all being true to themselves? Is it because all around us there are people who influence us to conform – conform to a 'brand', a model, an image, of which they approve? Some parent, some friend, some boss, some group culture, some aspiration which is not ours but is being attached to us from outside, some club for which the membership fee is conformity?

It is for us to work out for ourselves how much that 'membership' is worth, and to weigh it against the loss of that part of us which may have just died.

Read any of Shakespeare's biographers and you are left with more questions than answers. We know that he was born in 1564 and died in 1616 – after that you are into serious scholarly argument! Was his father, John, a closet Catholic? Was Anne Hathaway pregnant when they married? Were both his parents illiterate – else why did they sign with a mark instead of a name? Were the grieving passages in Twelfth Night *and* Hamlet *influenced by the recent death of his son, Hamnet? Did flattering references to the Earl of Essex put Will's life in danger when the Earl attempted a coup in 1601?*

Since he wrote at times in collaboration with other writers – anticipating by four hundred years the team-writing now commonly used to produce soap operas – how much of what we now have in his name is authentically his?

What awful thing did he do to Robert Greene, a contemporary author, who called him 'an upstart crow, beautified with our feathers...' Why did he leave his wife his 'second best bed'?

And, finally, did he die following a bout of binge drinking as described thus: 'Shakespeare, Drayton and Ben Jonson had a merry meeting and, it seems, drank too hard, for Shakespeare died of a fervour there contracted'.

Perhaps you'll catch the urge to research him for yourself?

S h a k e s p e a r e

Postscript

Bringing this book together has been a joy – it's also been frustrating and at times it's taken us down blind alleys and into valleys where we wondered whether we were going in the right direction.

At other times it has given us the opportunity to step on the uplands and high slopes of greater minds. Reflecting on the words quoted in this book has brought richness and diversity into our lives.

In fact so much enjoyment has been gained in finding the quotations, selecting them, and then reflecting on them and what they mean to us (and by extension, maybe to you), coupled with the research into the lives of the writers, that we would recommend the whole process to you.

This activity brings its own rewards – you'll find yourself beginning to read with renewed interest in what the author is whispering to you. It may be that nothing will appeal to you in one book, but a couple or more things will jump to you from another.

Be ready – read with a notebook close by. If the passage you're reading whispers (or shouts!) to you then make a note of it. Make a note too, of where you were when you read it, and write down some brief thoughts as to what it means to you. Later on you can type it all out if you wish – but we can guarantee that, in time, the notebook will become a very special possession.

Already heading through a second notebook, I find the first has become a treasured book . In fact it is my favourite book, and it travels with me – particularly on long haul flights. It's a mix of a diary, a journal and a history of the books I've read, and the impact they have had on me.

So, why not find a notebook that you feel comfortable with – not too fine a one either as it's very difficult to write on pristine fine white paper in a beautifully bound book, with anything but a calligrapher's hand. But whatever the notebook that you choose, make a start and you will find new vistas opening up in your mind and something that will say a great deal about you, and your life will begin to take shape.

Who knows? Maybe something that you've read in this collection will be the first entry in your own notebook – that would make us very happy, and the fun that we've had in bringing this collection together would have been more than worthwhile!

Acknowledgements

The authors have made diligent efforts to locate the copyright owners of all the reprinted text that appears in this book, but some have not been located. In the event that an excerpt has been printed without permission, the copyright owner should contact the authors c/o Loose Chippings Books, The Paddocks, Back Ends, Chipping Campden, Gloucestershire. GL55 6AU. Due acknowledgement will gladly be given in future editions.

The authors gratefully acknowledge the kind permissions granted by the following organisations to reproduce extracts from their copyright material.

Rachel Carson: Pollinger Ltd London
Frances Cornford: Permission is given by the Trustees of the Frances Crofts Cornford Will Trust
Noel Coward: A&C Black Publishers Limited, London.
Robert Frost: 'The Road Not Taken', from The Poetry of Robert Frost edited by Edward Connery Lathem, published by Jonathan Cape. Reprinted by permission of The Random House Group.
Robert Graves: Carcanet Press Ltd, Manchester
Graham Greene: 'The Heart Of The Matter', David Higham Associates, London.
A P Herbert: A P Watt Ltd on behalf of the estate of Jocelyn Herbert, M T Perkins and Polly M V R Perkins.
Ted King: preText Publishers Ltd. Marina Da Gama, South Africa.
Helen Nearing: reprinted from Loving and Leaving the Good Life by Helen Nearing copyright 1992 used with permission from Chelsea Green Publishing Co. White River Junction, Vermont, USA.
Clive Sansom: from An English Year by Clive Sansom, published by Chatto and Windus, copyright of David Higham Associates Ltd. London.
Edith Sitwell: from Collected Poems published by Duckworth, copyright of David Higham Associates Ltd. London.
Rabindranath Tagore: Visva Bharati, Santiniketan, West Bengal.
Van Loon: Palgrave Macmillan, Basingstoke.
Tennessee Williams: Georges Borchardt Inc. New York.
Marianne Williamson: Reprinted by permission of HarperCollins Publishers Ltd. Copyright A Return To Love by Marianne Williamson.

Also from Loose Chippings Books

The Cheesemonger's Tales
A good read for all food and wine lovers

Not Dark Yet
A very funny book about cricket

Cool Is The Reaping
Poems of rural England

Diary of a Shropshire Lass
A delightful autobiography

The Harts of Chipping Campden
Essential reading for all who admire the town or fine silver

Keeping Afloat
A light hearted tale of exploits on the canals of France

Roy The Eagle
Children's Picture Story Book about how what makes us different brings us together

Full details from our website
www.loosechippings.org